Mindfulness
Meditations
for Depression

SOPHIE A. LAZARUS, PhD

Mindfulness Meditations for Depression

100 PRACTICES FOR
SOLACE AND SELF-COMPASSION

ROCKRIDGE
PRESS

Interior and Cover Designer: Carlos Esparza
Art Producer: Samantha Ulban
Editor: Erin Nelson
Production Manager: Michael Kay
Production Editor: Melissa Edeburn

All images used under license Freepik.com.

Author photo courtesy of Meghan Breedlove.

ISBN: Print 978-1-64739-817-0 | eBook 978-1-64739-492-9

R0

To all those who undertake this practice.

CONTENTS

When inspiration has become hidden,

when we feel ready to give up, this is

the time when healing can be found in

the tenderness of pain itself.

—Pema Chödrön, Buddhist teacher and author

INTRODUCTION

The path to mindfulness often begins with the experience of great suffering. For me, it was a long and painful history of family upheaval due to loss and addiction. It seemed like the harder I tried to fix things, the more frustration and hopelessness I felt. After many years of struggling to stay afloat amid relentless waves of conflict and pain, I was introduced to mindfulness. But I believe that the seed of mindfulness was present within me long before I started watering it with regular practice.

The tenets of mindfulness resonated deeply, even as I struggled to accept them: We cannot control everything; we especially cannot control other people. Pain is inevitable. Our attachment to things being a certain way creates even more suffering. For me, mindfulness confirmed the possibility that with practice, we could see past our attachments—beyond the human urge to control the uncontrollable. With mindfulness, we can begin to heal by becoming more aware of the deeply ingrained habits that add to our distress. We can learn to consciously address difficulties with greater kindness and compassion.

It reminds me of being at the beach with my older brother as a child. Afraid of being injured by the waves, I hesitated to go deeper into the water. Instead, I ended up standing right where the waves broke, bracing against them and being knocked down time after time. Finally, my brother convinced me to close my eyes and dive underneath a big wave. There it was. A taste of freedom. I could not control the powerful forces of the ocean, but I could decide how I responded. Through practice, I learned that allowing the water to wash over me felt a heck of a lot better than getting pummeled at the shoreline.

As my personal practice of mindfulness grew, so too did evidence for the benefits of mindfulness for mental and physical health. In 2014, my training in clinical psychology took me to Duke University Medical Center, where I had the opportunity to co-lead an eight-week mindfulness-based cognitive therapy (MBCT) group. MBCT focuses on the development of mindfulness to cope with depressive patterns of negative thinking and prevent future depressive relapse. I knew strong research backed this treatment, and I saw firsthand how transformative the practice was for individuals suffering from severe and long-standing depression.

This experience was the impetus for a shift in my career. I redirected my research and clinical efforts to uncovering the benefits of practicing mindfulness. I developed an MBCT program to support people finding their way through painful experiences, encouraging them to flourish through increased awareness. I also worked with mentors through the University of California, San Diego, to become certified to teach MBCT, and I learned more about how changing one's relationship to difficulty could create freedom and choice.

I am constantly learning from my patients about depression and how to overcome its insidious pull through practice, openness, and courage. Through them I've seen that mindfulness is not just about avoiding depression; it's about accessing the sweet and surprising realness of the present moment. When we use mindfulness practice as a tool to manage judgment, we see that all of our experiences can be rich and worthy. Today, tomorrow, and through every experience, both pleasant and painful, we have the capacity to work wisely with whatever comes our way.

HOW TO USE
THIS BOOK

This book is intended to support you in developing or deepening a practice of mindfulness. The hope is that through mindfulness, some of the unhelpful patterns of thinking and behavior that fuel low mood become clearer. With time, you might experiment with new ways of responding to these thoughts, using awareness to manage—or at least better understand—mood, anxiety, and well-being.

Each chapter is an invitation to explore how a core principle of mindfulness can help you work with the challenging patterns that come with depression. Within each chapter, meditations progress in difficulty, moving from foundational meditations to meditations that address troubling emotions and patterns of reactivity. My recommendation is to read each chapter from beginning to end. That said, you don't need to read the chapters in the order that they appear. It's best to concentrate on whichever chapter, or meditation, seems best suited to meet your needs at any given moment.

You can try one meditation daily. If you're struggling to begin, turn to any of the mini meditations that appear throughout the book. They are a quick but thoughtful way to ease into your mindfulness practice. Each meditation you'll find here fosters self-love and self-compassion. Cultivating these qualities is critical to caring for yourself as you begin to explore living with difficult experiences.

Meditation is challenging at the best of times. When depression is severe, it is natural to have trouble concentrating, and negative thoughts can feel particularly intense. During these times, be extra kind to yourself.

Although mindfulness and meditation tend to be helpful for most folks, they may not be right for everyone all the time. Mind your own limits by attending to your window of tolerance. You might think of this window as the zone in which you are able to safely explore your experience, even if it is difficult. In this zone, you can learn. Outside the zone, emotions may be so intense that you can no longer be receptive to new information. If you notice yourself moving outside your zone, step away and do something to take care of yourself. You might open your eyes, take a few deep breaths, or step away to have some water or tea. While part of mindfulness practice is about learning how to relate to difficulty in a new way, it is also important to know when to make modifications to your mindfulness practice to honor your limits.

As you begin your practice, remember the instructions for each meditation are an invitation rather than a command. If any portion of the practice becomes too intense, you can always come back to the breath or feel your feet on the ground to refocus your attention. No matter how you adapt your practice, you are learning something valuable about yourself and how to manage your thoughts and emotions.

This book is not a replacement for seeking treatment for depression. If symptoms of depression begin to cause serious distress or affect your ability to cope with home life, work life, or other people, you should seek treatment from a mental health professional. You can find local resources through FindTreatment.SAMHSA.gov.

Heart pain and mind pain are great teachers,

showing us the path to compassionate action.

This is the life of the spiritual warrior.

—Tias Little, author and yoga instructor

CHAPTER ONE

Mindfulness for Depression

If you picked up this book because you struggle with depression, you are not alone. According to the Centers for Disease Control and Prevention, depression is one of the most common mental disorders. At any given time, 8 percent of adults in the United States deal with it. Whether or not you have experienced a major depressive episode, depression is a human experience that touches all of us.

PATTERNS OF DEPRESSION

We all experience loss, rejection, loneliness, and disappointment. Sometimes these emotions pass quickly. Other times they linger and worsen, causing problems with sleep, appetite, energy, and concentration and even feelings of hopelessness and guilt and thoughts of suicide. When these problems start to interfere with your ability to take care of yourself, work, and participate in relationships, they may rise to the level of clinical depression. Like other common disorders, depression has a universal set of symptoms and a number of evidence-based treatments.

Although it is important to acknowledge that depression is a common illness with a known set of symptoms, it is also true that part of the insidious nature of depression is that it feels deeply personal and isolating. Once depression has taken hold, symptoms of depression like fatigue, lack of motivation, and trouble with decision-making are often taken as character flaws rather than indicators that someone needs help. Despite the fact that effective treatments for depression do exist, 35 percent of adults who experienced a major depressive episode in the past year did not seek treatment. Imagine that statistic being true for another serious health issue, like heart disease or asthma.

We will address the patterns that make it hard to care for ourselves in this book.

The Shadow of Your Thoughts

Our thoughts and beliefs about a situation have a powerful effect on us. An inner commentary filled with judging, comparing, and evaluating often leaves us discouraged and unmotivated. Left unchecked, negative thoughts and beliefs can leave us vulnerable to low moods that spiral downward.

Meditation teacher and author Ram Dass described negative thoughts this way: "We're sitting under the tree of our thinking minds, wondering why we're not getting any sunshine!" Through mindfulness, we gain awareness of the tree—our thoughts and emotions, and the urges that come along with them—and we can choose how we want to respond. We open up the possibility of stepping out into the sunshine.

Getting Unstuck from Emotions

As human beings, we tend to deal with negative feelings in one of two ways. We may just ignore the problem and try to suppress the feelings. Or we may get stuck trying to think our way out of the problem. We may ask ourselves, "What's wrong with me that I feel so unhappy all the time?"

Patterns of emotional avoidance and suppression often lead to behaviors that further exacerbate our mood. Similarly, ruminating on our feelings is an understandable impulse, but it rarely leads to some brilliant solution. Instead, it creates a harmful spiral that immobilizes us—mentally and physically. As our thinking takes up all of our attention, at the expense of our experience, problems seem even more insurmountable, and we get stuck. We are so wrapped up in needing to feel different that we are unable to take the actions that might help us.

Through mindfulness, we can bring a sense of curiosity to discovering our own unique mental ruts that keep us stuck. This awareness is an important step toward choosing a different path.

The Trap of Avoidance

Major life changes, especially traumatic events, can take us away from sources of positive emotion and reinforcement. When we're depleted, our typical ways of dealing with stress and negative emotions can break down.

Often, we turn to avoidance to cope. Avoidance can look different for different people—oversleeping, using alcohol, shopping excessively, or zoning out on our phone for hours. No matter the presentation of these avoidant patterns, they make it hard to recover. Although turning to them might help temporarily, these behaviors also tend to take us further from what we truly want.

Even seemingly helpful strategies can become counterproductive when they are really about avoiding difficult emotions. For example, taking extra time to make sure everything is "perfect" can seem like a good thing, until you stop doing things you enjoy in order to put absolute perfection first. Over time, the strategy that once worked backfires and leads to exhaustion and isolation. With mindfulness, we can become more aware of the critical relationship between our mood and our behavior, and we can use that information to make changes to better care for ourselves.

WHAT IS MINDFULNESS?

We all have moments on autopilot. These are the moments when our attention has been hijacked by our own thinking. Have you ever arrived home from work or school without remembering how you got there? Or finished an entire meal in front of the computer or TV without knowing how it tasted? When the mind is doing one thing while the body is doing another, we often feel like we're just going through the motions. We are literally lost in thought, anticipating the future or rehashing the past.

This state can wreak havoc on our moods. Are you anticipating a positive future outcome? Or are you worrying about being hurt or failing in some way? It's rare that we replay a great success.

Mindfulness is the process of getting back in the driver's seat of our awareness. It is about refocusing on the present moment, practicing seeing your experience more clearly, and doing so with kindness and compassion. Scientist, author, and meditation teacher Jon Kabat-Zinn defines mindfulness as "paying attention in a particular way: on purpose, in the present moment, and nonjudgmentally."

You can be mindful of anything that is happening in the present moment—sensations, passing thoughts, sounds, sights, emotions, and smells. Fundamentally, mindfulness is not about relaxing, clearing the mind, or even changing anything. It teaches us to wake up to the present moment. This awareness not only allows us to actually inhabit our lives but also introduces the possibility of responding wisely to difficulty rather than reacting habitually. As one patient described it to me, "This practice can help me live life and not have my negative thoughts control me."

Luckily, research has shown us that mindfulness is a skill that can be cultivated through practice. Daily practice of mindfulness can enhance well-being, mental health, physical health, and interpersonal relationships. Critically for us, interventions based on mindfulness have been shown to help reduce symptoms of depression and reduce the risk of relapse once someone is well. We have also learned that even brief periods of guided mindfulness, especially when practiced regularly, can have benefits for mood and mental health. In other words, you don't have to sit for hours a day or be an experienced meditator to benefit from mindfulness practice. All you have to do is begin.

The 7 Principles of Mindfulness

We know that mindfulness involves paying attention, but this is only part of the picture. *How* we pay attention and the attitudes we bring to this attention also influence our experience. Imagine that when you sit down to practice, you are watering the seed of mindfulness. Your attitude is the sun, a key ingredient for the seed to grow.

The following principles are often described as the pillars or foundations of mindfulness. Focusing on cultivating these principles creates the conditions for awareness and compassion to flourish. As you will see, this book is structured around these principles because they can directly counteract the negative, self-critical, and hopeless thought patterns that fuel depression.

BEGINNER'S MIND is the *intention* to see each experience with fresh eyes. Rather than letting our ideas and expectations color how we see things, beginner's mind lets curiosity help us see the reality of each moment.

NON-JUDGMENT is the *intention* to be more mindful of judgments that arise and not judge ourselves for judging. Even though it is completely normal and sometimes quicker to judge something as good or bad, or fair or unfair, these ideas often become filters through which we see the world and increase reactivity and rumination. Practicing non-judgment allows for greater clarity and wisdom.

ACCEPTANCE is the *intention* to put out the welcome mat for whatever arises, regardless of whether we like it. Acceptance does not mean that we have to give in or resign ourselves to whatever happens, but rather that we actively choose to recognize what is—and use that as a starting place for wise action.

PATIENCE is the *intention* to inhabit the present moment and allow everything to unfold in its own time. The truth is, some things cannot be hurried. Rushing around and missing the moment doesn't often benefit us as much as we anticipate.

TRUST is the *intention* to honor your experience and your own inherent goodness. Rather than looking outside yourself for how you should feel, trust is looking inside yourself to understand how you actually feel. To be yourself, understand yourself, and honor yourself is to trust.

NON-STRIVING is the *intention* to shift from doing to being. We are always trying to get somewhere and accomplish something, and this attitude often causes more tension and stress. Non-striving allows us to be ourselves, because regardless of whether we accept it, we already are.

LETTING GO is the *intention* to notice the ways that holding on too tightly keeps us stuck. The mind often clings to experiences we deem desirable and rejects experiences we deem undesirable. Because much of life is out of our control, this way of thinking can be a trap. Letting go is acknowledging how things are, including our desire for them to be different, without getting swept away.

The truth is that paying attention when things are unpleasant is hard. Our natural tendency is to shut down, avoid, or suppress things that hurt to confront. The pillars of mindfulness provide us with a safe way of paying attention that can hold even the most painful thoughts, feelings, and sensations.

What Is Mindfulness-Based Cognitive Therapy?

Mindfulness-based cognitive therapy (MBCT) is a powerful application of mindfulness that was developed to help those who experience recurrent episodes of depression and chronic unhappiness. MBCT combines mindfulness and elements of cognitive therapy to support greater awareness and skill in working with depressive patterns of thinking. In an MBCT program, participants meet as a group once per week over a period of two months and practice mindfulness. The participants cultivate a new relationship to the modes of mind that contribute to depression and anxiety.

Significant research has shown the positive effects MBCT can have on depression, anxiety, and numerous other mental health problems. Mindfulness can address patterns that get us stuck, and so the writings and meditations found in this book will touch on many of the core principles, themes, and practices of MBCT. At the same time, as mentioned earlier, this book is not a substitute for professional help. Especially when you're depressed, the support structure of an MBCT program and the guidance of a professional can be invaluable. You can find providers of MBCT at AccessMBCT.com.

WHAT IS MEDITATION?

We have already discussed mindfulness, which is a certain quality of attention that we can bring to the present moment. Mindfulness can be practiced informally and brought into our daily life by fully engaging in a meal or a conversation. It can also be practiced through periods of formal meditation.

In meditation, time is set aside to deliberately practice bringing attention to the present moment, typically using some anchor like the breath, body, or sounds. In this book, we will focus primarily on mindfulness meditations to support greater control of attention and awareness of habits of the mind. However, there will be exercises in which you are asked to bring mindfulness into your daily life to attend to unhelpful patterns as they arise. You may see mindfulness and meditation as two sides of the same coin. Mindfulness deepens meditation, and meditation expands mindfulness.

A JOURNEY OF SELF-COMPASSION

The 100 meditations here are intended to help you develop a greater awareness of your own present moment, no matter what that moment is. Noticing and gently acknowledging what is actually happening, without judgment, can be healing all on its own. Remember, there is no particular goal here. As strange as it may seem now, we are not trying to clear our mind, get rid of thoughts, or even feel happier. Difficult thoughts and emotions are part of being alive. What we are cultivating is a willingness to be with all thoughts, feelings, and sensations as they arise and pass. The greatest "achievement" would be to bring a sense of kindness and curiosity to whatever you notice as you go through these exercises.

A little bit of self-compassion goes a long way here. Know that now you are part of a community of mindfulness practitioners, and we are all on our own unique version of the same path.

As longtime meditation teacher and author Sharon Salzberg has said, "Mindfulness isn't difficult; we just need to remember to do it." That is, if we trust for the time being that mindfulness is truly a practice rather than a destination, then the challenge is really about remembering to do it on a daily basis. We have all spent years on autopilot, creating well-worn mental and behavioral ruts. It is going to take time and practice to see those patterns clearly and make space to choose something different.

Although mindfulness may not be difficult, it is courageous to let go of habitual and often comfortable patterns of avoiding, suppressing, and distracting. To look inward can be scary. In truth, we often come to this path when we begin to realize that our old ways of coping aren't working.

By embarking on this path, you are beginning to water the seed of mindfulness that exists within you. What a caring act! Remember not to rush. Choose a pace that works for you. You don't need to complete all the meditations at once. Rather, spend some time with each chapter to practice and notice how the theme applies to your life. Then let that theme go and move on. There is no need to drown the seed, and there may be periods of drought. Just keep tending to the seed little by little, and something surprising will emerge.

The art of living in this "predicament" is neither careless drifting on the one hand nor fearful clinging to the past and the known on the other. It consists in being completely sensitive to each moment, in regarding it as utterly new and unique, in having the mind open and wholly receptive.

—Alan Watts, author and speaker

CHAPTER TWO

Beginner's Mind

Thoughts and ideas from our past or predictions of the future often form a filter through which we see the world. This perspective leaves little room for new information to get through. We move through our day dwelling on the unknown future or the settled past, rather than observing what *is*.

A familiar wave of sadness arises, and the mind starts spinning: *Oh no, it's happening again. What is wrong with me that I can't just be happy? Is it always going to be this way? I should probably stay home because I won't be any fun.* This torrent of negative thoughts fuels emotions that then drive behaviors that take us further from the present moment and deeper into depression. A beginner's mind can free us from this trap.

Beginner's mind involves an attitude of openness—removing the filters, ideas, and expectations that color how we see things. It is an attitude of not knowing that allows us to see our experience with greater clarity and less reactivity. Imagine experiencing the moment as a child would, with a blank slate and a strong sense of curiosity. *Hmm, what does sadness feel like? How does it change and shift? Perhaps sadness is just sadness.* When we let go of what sadness might mean and simply notice how it feels, the experience can unfold naturally, and we avoid getting so stuck. Beginner's mind keeps us open where depression shuts us down.

Common Unhelpful Thoughts

> *This is never going to end.*
> *This is going to be just like the time before.*
> *I won't enjoy it, so why even try?*

---

1. ARRIVE WHERE YOU ARE

🕐 5 minutes

Often, the mind is either ten steps ahead, trying to figure out what's next, or a few steps behind, replaying what just happened. The first step in mindfulness is arriving where you are. This meditation is intended to bring the body and the mind together in the same place. Use this meditation to gather and steady your attention.

- Wherever you are, start by sitting up in your seat with your back straight and relaxed, feet on the floor. Allow your eyes to gently close, or cast your gaze softly on the floor.
- Start by tuning in to your feet. Feel the feet where they rest on the ground. Notice any sensations.
- Guide your attention to the sensations in your thighs and buttocks, wherever the body meets the surface where you are sitting. Feel the weight of the body being held and supported by the chair.

- Shift your attention to your back. Notice the sensations where the back meets the chair and where it does not.
- Turn your attention to your hands. Feel where the hands rest or where they touch each other. What do they feel like in this moment?
- Finally, feel your whole body sitting here. Gently breathe with a sense of the whole body, in this moment. If your attention wanders off, gently bring your attention back to feeling the body, however your body is right now.
- As you finish this meditation, know you can always arrive just where you are by noticing your body and the body's points of contact—with the earth, with a chair, with itself.

2. DISCOVER YOUR BREATH

🕐 10 minutes

We are always breathing, yet we are rarely aware of it. In this practice, you will discover your breath as if you were feeling it for the first time. Each breath is a new breath to explore with interest and curiosity. As Buddhist scholar and activist Thich Nhat Hanh has said, "Our breathing is a stable solid ground that we can take refuge in. No matter what is going on inside us—thoughts, emotions, or perceptions—our breathing is always with us, like a faithful friend."

- Begin this practice by finding a quiet place to sit. Sit in a way that feels comfortable, awake, and upright. Your eyes may be closed or open, depending on your preference.
- Take a few moments to notice the sensations of sitting, feeling the points of contact where your body meets the surface you are sitting on.
- As you sit, start to become aware of the fact that you are breathing. Allow the breath to be natural, and let the body breathe all on its own.

(CONTINUED)

- Start by exploring the sensations of the breath at the belly. Feel the belly rise on the inhale and fall on the exhale. Take a few moments to carefully feel each new breath with your full attention.
- If you become aware of thoughts arising, see whether you can gently acknowledge "thinking," then return to feeling the sensations of breathing.
- Now move your attention to feel the breath at the chest. Feel the chest inflating on the inhale and deflating on the exhale.
- When you are ready, shift to investigate the sensations of the breath at the nostrils. Feel the cool air come in and the warm air go out. Carefully discover each new breath.
- For a few breaths, feel the whole length of the breath in the body as it moves through the nostrils, chest, and belly.
- As this meditation comes to an end, take a moment to consider the uniqueness of each breath.

3. TEMPERATURE CHECK

🕐 10 minutes

Just as a thermometer tells our temperature, the body can be an indicator of our state of mind. Checking in with our body allows us to see how things are and attend to what may be needed. In this practice we move through a gentle scan of places where we often hold tension. Rather than judging or evaluating what we find, the intention is simply to notice.

- Find a comfortable seat where you feel at ease and awake. You can also practice this meditation lying on your back if you are not too sleepy. If you are on your back, allow your arms to lie alongside your body with palms up. Gently close your eyes, or keep them open with your gaze soft.
- Start by turning your attention to your face. What sensations do you notice in the face right now? Feel any tightness or tingling, and continue to breathe as you observe any sensations that arise.
- If you find yourself thinking about the body, see whether you can

come back to directly sensing it. Know that if any sensations become too overwhelming or uncomfortable, you can always shift your attention back to the breath or somewhere in the body that feels more neutral or pleasant.

- Shift your attention to your shoulders. What sensations are present in the shoulders in this moment? Notice any tension or temperature as you breathe, and be aware of sensations as they move, shift, or stay the same.
- Let your attention move to your belly. What sensations can you detect in the belly?
- Guide your attention to your hands. What sensations do you notice in the hands in this moment? Breathe with whatever sensations arise.
- Finally, take a few breaths to tune in to the body as a whole. Feel the changing pattern of sensations in the body as you breathe. Allow the body to be just as it is.
- As you complete this practice, gently open your eyes. Bring some gentle movement back into your body.

4. MINDFUL LISTENING

🕐 5 minutes

With a beginner's mind, we meet each new moment precisely as it is. When we are open to each moment, we can notice our "expert" thinking mind and how it takes us out of the flow of really listening, instead bringing us to judgment or explanation. This practice is one of letting go of thinking and coming back to mindful listening. You can do this meditation any time that you have a few moments alone.

- Start by sitting in an attentive and comfortable position. Take a few deep breaths and let your body settle to the degree it will. Let your eyes close.
- Now turn your attention to the ears and begin to open up to the sounds around you. Notice sounds that are nearby and far away, quiet and loud.

(CONTINUED)

- See whether you can have an attitude of curiosity and openness as you listen. Instead of seeking out sounds, see whether you can allow sounds to arrive at the ears.
- Each time you become aware that you are thinking about sounds, remembering, or planning, gently label what you are doing as "thinking" and direct your attention back to the sounds.
- Observe the way sounds arise and fade away.
- Notice when your attention drifts, and without judgment or too much inner discussion, let go and come back to listening. Try to relax into the reality of not knowing what sounds will arise next, how long they will last, or whether you will find them pleasant or unpleasant. (A true beginner's mind!)
- As this practice ends, slowly open all your senses to the present moment.

5. FRESH PERSPECTIVE

(Mini-Meditation)

Every time you wash your hands throughout the day, use this time as an opportunity to bring your full attention to your senses. Notice how the water feels on your hands. Feel the temperature and texture as you lather the soap. Tune in to any smells or sounds that arise. Allow this moment of mindfulness in the busyness of your day to nourish you.

6. BEING BEHIND YOUR EYES

🕐 5 minutes

When I was first trying to understand what mindfulness was, I thought of it as being behind my eyes. I often felt that when I got pulled into thinking, I disappeared and started to miss out on the moment. When I somehow unhooked from thinking and came back to the present, I felt like I was back behind my eyes, seeing what was in front of me. This exercise can be done looking out a window or anywhere with a view.

- Standing at the window, take a moment to feel your feet on the ground. Feel a breath or two, just getting grounded in the moment.
- Now bring your attention to seeing what is in front of you. Let your gaze take in everything, seeing it as if for the first time.
- Take in the raw color, texture, and patterns. Carefully receive the sights in front of you, remaining fully aware.
- See whether you can take in the sights rather than thinking about them. See each detail of what is before you. If you notice that you are getting pulled away from seeing, gently let go and return to being behind your eyes.
- If thoughts or judgments arise beyond neutrally noting what you see, gently label those thoughts "thinking," and guide your attention back to seeing.
- As this practice comes to an end, gently widen your gaze. Remember that you can always use the sights in front of you to anchor you in the present moment.

7. NO TWO BREATHS ARE THE SAME

🕐 1 to 2 minutes (repeat)

No two breaths are the same. When we look at the breath this way, we can bring renewed attention and interest to our breath. Set the intention to become aware of your breath periodically throughout the day. Try to link this practice with something you do regularly, like having a drink of water or getting up from your desk. We'll use the example of taking a sip of water.

- Each time you have a sip of water, take a moment to find your breath. Notice your breath wherever it feels clearest to you—at your nose, your chest, or your belly.

(CONTINUED)

- Ask yourself what your breath feels like right now. Observe the sensations.
- Bring a sense of curiosity to the breath, noticing whether it is deep or shallow, quick or slow, rough or smooth.
- Follow the breath for a few moments. Without judgment, notice whether it changes or stays the same. Perhaps say to yourself, *Ah, that is how it is right now.*
- Gently let go of the breath. Take a sip of water and return to the flow of your day.
- Next time you take a drink of water, repeat this exercise.
- At the end of the day, reflect on what you observed about your breath throughout your day.

---

8. EXPLORING SCENT

🕐 5 minutes

One of my most beloved mindfulness teachers is my dog, Millie. Each time we step outside for a walk, she throws her head back and wildly sniffs the air. Day after day, year after year, she is excited and curious to discover what is out there. For the following meditation, choose something that you frequently drink or eat, like a cup of coffee or some type of fruit. We will be exploring scent with the intention to experience the newness of each moment.

- Sit upright with your chosen item in front of you on a table. Place your hands in your lap.
- Close your eyes and take a few deep breaths. Feel the breath come in and out.
- Take a moment to imagine that this item is completely new to you. (Note that you have never had *this* cup of tea before.) Invite an attitude of curiosity as you open your eyes and take the item in your hands.

- Gently bring the item under your nose, and continue to breathe with your eyes open. Allow any aroma to simply arrive at your nose as you breathe.
- If you find yourself pulled into thinking or caught up in some storyline, just gently let go and guide your attention back to your nose, back to the sensation of smell.
- Continue to breathe and observe what you smell, how it changes, and anything else that happens in your body as you do this.
- Allow your eyes to gently close. Continue to hold this item under your nose as you breathe. Observe any scent arising from this object. Notice any fading or intensifying as you continue to breathe.
- Finally, place the object down and breathe for a few moments in the absence of this object under your nose. Notice the sensations of breathing and any remaining scents that arise.

9. ROUTINE AWARENESS

🕐 Once per day

When our mood is low, life can start to seem dull. We lose our sense of interest and put things on autopilot to conserve what feels like very limited energy. The problem is that on autopilot, we are very unlikely to notice anything interesting, pleasant, or uplifting. This exercise invites us to see what happens when we bring a fresh perspective to a routine activity or bleak state of mind.

- For one week, choose a routine activity that you plan to be mindful of. Activities like showering, brushing your teeth, drinking your coffee, or washing the dishes are usually accessible choices.
- Set the intention to approach this activity with beginner's mind, noticing the actual experience of it. You might need to set a reminder or an alarm to stay consistent.

(CONTINUED)

- As you perform your routine activity, see whether you can bring your full attention to your senses.
- Aim to slow down a bit, taking in the sights, smells, and sensations.
- As old habits arise and you get pulled into autopilot, intentionally unhook from thinking. Come back to your senses to take in the fullness of the experience. Be open to what you notice.
- Repeat this with the same activity daily.
- Reflect on what it was like to do this this activity in this new way. Choose a new activity to complete mindfully the following week.

---

10. EXPLORING A MINDFUL MORSEL

🕐 10 minutes

Eating is one of the most common things we do automatically. It is easy to eat and do something else at the same time—and it is easy to miss the whole experience. A beginner's mind can bring a whole new sense of satisfaction and appreciation to the experience of eating. In this exercise, choose a food such as a raisin, a berry, or a small piece of chocolate. Try to approach this exercise as a child might take a bite of something brand-new.

- Take a seat where you can have some quiet and privacy. Sit up straight and allow your body to relax with your feet flat on the floor.
- Hold whatever food you chose in your palm with your hand closed.
- Gently close your eyes or cast your gaze on the floor. Feel the chair beneath you, and notice the sensations of sitting here.
- Now open your eyes and your hand. Begin by exploring this morsel with your sense of vision. Carefully examine it as if you have never seen it before. Turn it over in your palm to see it from all sides.
- Explore this morsel with your sense of touch. Notice its weight in your palm and how it feels on your fingers and hands. See whether you can gently let go of thinking and direct your attention back to feeling this morsel.

- Take this morsel between two fingers and bring it under your nose. Explore it with your sense of smell.
- Bring this morsel to your ear and explore it with your sense of hearing. Move it around between your fingers and notice any sounds.
- Each time you notice your attention has wandered, guide it back.
- Bring this morsel to your lips and notice the intention to place it in your mouth before doing so.
- Allow this morsel to be in your mouth without chewing. Explore how it feels in your mouth, noticing any flavors or urges that arise.
- Now, with your full awareness, bite down and very slowly begin to chew. Observe any tastes, textures, or changes as you chew.
- Do you feel the urge to finish your bite? Detect the intention to swallow before doing so. Notice all that has to happen in your mouth in order to swallow.
- As this practice comes to an end, take a moment to once again notice how your mouth feels in the absence of food.

11. UNHOOK

🕐 10 minutes

One of the trickiest parts of depression is that once we have experienced it, we can easily become fearful of relapsing and spiral into negative thinking at any hints of its possible return. Unfortunately, this cycle of predicting, blaming, and remembering can almost ensure that things get worse. Our task is to learn to work wisely with this reactivity. One way to do so is to purposefully unhook from thinking and instead be with feelings as they arise in the body. In this way, we are not avoiding or suppressing but bravely being with the moment.

- Begin this practice by finding a comfortable seated posture. You can let your eyes close or softly cast your gaze downward.
- Take a moment to settle into your seat and notice where your body makes contact with the chair or cushion.

(CONTINUED)

- Shift your attention to rest on the breath. Carefully follow the sensations of the breath wherever they are clearest to you.
- After a time, you will notice thinking. Whenever you become aware of thinking, gently let go and return to the breath.
- If you become aware of the mind being pulled to a particularly sticky thought or worry, now you can try something different. Take a few moments to shift your attention to the body. As you shift your attention, see whether you can detect any sensations of tension, holding, or bracing. If you do, allow yourself time to anchor your attention to these sensations as you breathe. Observe them with curiosity and kindness.
- If the sensations no longer call for your attention, feel free to let go and return to simply following your breath.
- Allow yourself to continue in this way. If you get caught up in difficult thoughts, gently unhook from thinking and instead focus on feeling the body.
- As this practice ends, congratulate yourself for exploring this different way of being with challenging thoughts.

12. COMFORT IN UNCERTAINTY

🕐 10 minutes

When faced with uncertainty or discomfort, we often get caught up in needing to know how things are going to turn out or what is going to happen. In reality, we can't know. By acknowledging this truth, we can begin to free ourselves from compulsive thinking and worrying. This is a practice taught by meditation teacher Jack Kornfield. Try it when you are feeling relatively settled rather than upset or stressed.

- Sit quietly for a time, with an upright and relaxed posture. Allow your eyes to gently close.
- Take a few moments to simply feel the length of each inhale and each exhale.

- When you are ready, bring to mind a time in the future, perhaps five years from now. Imagine what this time is like. Now acknowledge that as much as you may have plans and ideas about the future, you don't really know what will happen and what the future will be like. Repeat to yourself, *I don't know*. Notice the feelings of not knowing and kindly breathe with them.
- Now think about some of the great mysteries of this earth, of all the people being born and dying each day. Where does life come from, and where does it go? Notice how much we don't know. Repeat to yourself, *I don't know*. Sense your "don't know" mind, and gently allow your body to relax with whatever you notice.
- If it feels safe, allow inner or outer conflict to enter your mind. Take note of all of the thoughts and opinions you hold about what is fair or how things should be. Again, acknowledge that you really don't know. Perhaps things not going "right" will lead to something surprising, worthwhile, or deeply fulfilling.
- Consider for a moment how we might be limited by what we think we know. What would it be like to bring the "don't know" mind to new situations, to ourselves, and to other to people?
- See if you can bring a bit of this "don't know" mind to situations in which there is uncertainty. Take a deep breath and do your best to laugh, saying to yourself, *I don't know*.

---

13. INVESTIGATING EXPECTATIONS

◷ Ongoing   ✎ pen and paper

Have you ever had a thought or worry that didn't come true? *I'll never be able to get it all done. Everyone will notice my bad haircut.* Our expectations and ideas about a situation can have a strong influence on our experience, even if they never come true. With mindfulness, we can become aware of our expectations

(CONTINUED)

so they have less of a grip over us. Rather than being driven by ideas and predictions, we can see the moment clearly and respond to whatever arises with skill and wisdom.

- Choose a day when you may face some stress or challenges. As you wake up and begin your day, carefully notice what thoughts come up. Bring a sense of curiosity to expectations or predictions as they present themselves.
- Approach your thoughts without judgment. Simply notice and perhaps record what you become aware of.
- Continue to remain aware of expectations and predictions as you prepare for your day.
- Throughout the day, and especially when preparing to transition to a new or challenging activity or conversation, see whether you can notice the expectations that arise. See whether you can simply take note of the expectations, write them down, and go on with your day.
- Complete this practice two more times on days when you anticipate facing some difficulty or stress.
- Take some time to reflect on what you observed during your investigation. Notice whether this practice was helpful in becoming more aware or releasing the grip of your expectations. If so, continue this practice.

14. FEELING LANDSCAPES

🕐 10 minutes

In this meditation, we invite that possibility that emotions are meant to be felt rather than solved. For many of us, getting to know what emotions actually feel like is the first step to this radical act of feeling feelings. Often what we call a "feeling" is made up of emotions (like sadness), sensations (such as heaviness in the chest), and urges (like wanting to sleep). Getting to know the landscape of our feelings can help us avoid being overwhelmed by them. Try this meditation when you become aware of some *minor* difficulty, irritation, disappointment, or worry.

- Start this practice by finding a comfortable and quiet place to sit. Adopt a posture that is alert and awake to the present moment. Gently close your eyes, or let your gaze fall softly to the floor.
- Begin to turn your attention inward, taking note of how the body feels. Gently tune in to any sensation of tension, holding, or tightness in the body. See whether you can do this with a sense of exploration rather than fixing.
- Turn your attention to noticing any emotions that are present. Simply detect any emotion—anxiety, frustration, or sadness—rather than thinking about the emotion, why it is present, or how to get rid of it.
- Begin to notice any thoughts that come along with the difficulty that you were aware of when you began this meditation. See whether you can observe the thoughts that arise and let them pass through the mind. You can label them: anxious thought, self-critical thought, or thought about the future.
- Perhaps say to yourself, *Ah, this is how it feels right now.*
- Bring your attention back to the breath. Allow the sensations of the breath to anchor you in this moment.
- As this practice comes to an end, take a few moments to congratulate yourself for approaching your experience in this different way. You've demonstrated an attitude of bravery and a beginner's mind.

Words of Encouragement

Inviting a beginner's mind into each moment takes practice. Remember that there is no right or wrong way for meditations to unfold. Focus on the process rather than the outcome. Whatever your experience, that is exactly what you are invited to notice.

Reflection

What did you notice as you worked through these meditations? What aspects of your experience stood out? How can you apply the attitude of beginner's mind to your daily life?

Mindfulness Meditations for Depression

We must put down our prejudices and live in the world with the sky, the trees, the air, and other people.

—Seung Sahn, founder of the Kwan Um School of Zen

CHAPTER THREE

Non-judgment

We often use judgment as shorthand to state our preferences. Instead of saying, "I don't enjoy this flavor," we might say, "This is gross." Judgment becomes a problem when we forget that our judgments are personal opinions based on individual experiences. Without this awareness, judgment tends to hook us into patterns of resistance and reactivity.

Take a moment to imagine that a coworker gets a promotion you hoped for. Feel the difference between "That is very disappointing; I really wanted that promotion" and "That is so unfair; this is totally ridiculous." Judgment can transform an emotional challenge into a stalemate. The more we resist and fight against reality, the deeper we sink into debilitating disappointment and anger.

With non-judgment, we can observe the facts of a situation and our reaction to it—including any judgments—with clarity and a bit of space.

Instead of judging ourselves for judging, we can pause, notice what is happening, and decide how to respond. We can still notice preferences or communicate needs. In fact, with non-judgment, we'll probably get closer to what we want. Cultivating non-judgment helps us open up to greater understanding, wisdom, and discernment. Non-judgment is a radical act of kindness that can support us in responding wisely to the challenges before us.

Common Unhelpful Thoughts

We know judgment is around when our inner commentary includes words like "should," "shouldn't," "right," "wrong," "fair," "unfair," "good," "bad," "better," "best," and "worst."

> *This shouldn't be so hard.*
>
> *I deserve this because I'm lazy.*
>
> *Everyone else seems to be doing better than I am.*

---

15. ALLOW THE BREATH TO BE

🕐 10 minutes

Breath is a common anchor for practicing mindfulness. Coming back to the breath can provide a powerful way to unhook from our thoughts and ground ourselves, even if only for a moment. It is easy to get pulled into judgments about how our breath "should" be. In this practice, we work with allowing the breath to be just as it is.

- Begin by sitting upright in a comfortable position. Allow your shoulders to relax back and down so your chest is open and your breath can flow naturally. Gently close your eyes or rest your gaze downward.
- Take three slightly deeper breaths, and as you do this, see where you can detect the breath most clearly in the body.

- Let the breath resume its natural rhythm, and begin to attend to the sensations of breathing wherever they feel most apparent or pleasant. You might focus on the nostrils, the chest, or the belly.
- Feel the breath as it enters and leaves your body. Bring your full attention to the sensations of the breath.
- As you breathe, notice whether any judgments about your breath arise. If any do arise, gently label them "judgment," and come back to noticing each breath. See whether you can celebrate the act of noticing when judgment arises.
- There is no need to change or control the breath. Allow the breath to be just as it is in this moment.
- If other thoughts or judgments arise, feel free to gently label them "judgment" or "thinking," and simply guide your attention back to observing the changing sensations as you breathe.
- As this practice comes to an end, take a moment to connect with a sense of gratitude for your efforts to allow the breath to be.

16. YOUR BODY IS BEAUTIFUL

🕐 15 minutes

We rarely take time to appreciate all our body does to help us move, create, carry, speak, and sense the world around us. When things are going well, we take our body for granted, and yet we always notice something wrong, like an illness or injury. Perhaps even more adhesive are the ideas we hold about how our body should look or be. But as Jon Kabat-Zinn urges us, remember that "as long as you are breathing, there is more right with you than there is wrong."

- Find a quiet place to sit upright or lie down. If you lie down, allow your legs to be long, with your feet falling away from each other. Let your arms be alongside your body, with the palms up. Allow your eyes to gently close, or let your gaze remain unfocused.

(CONTINUED)

- Take some time to feel the sensations of the body. Notice the points of contact where the body meets the mat or the chair. Feel the whole length of the body.
- Remember that the intention of this body scan is to directly feel the sensations as you move your attention through the body. There is no right or wrong way to feel, and there is no need to relax or feel any different. See whether you can forgo judgment about what you should feel and simply notice what is there. As thoughts arise during the body scan, see whether you can take note of thinking and gently return to the body.
- When you are ready, move your attention down your legs into the feet. Begin by exploring sensations in the toes, the soles of the feet, and the tops of the feet.
- Shift your attention to your ankles and lower legs. Feel sensations arising from the skin and deep inside the lower legs. If there are no sensations, that is okay. Just rest your attention in the lower legs.
- Shift your attention up to the knees and upper legs. Notice any temperature or pressure. Gently let go of thinking about the sensations and directly feel them.
- Bring your attention to the region of the pelvis. Notice any sensations that arise as you breathe. If any thoughts or emotions arise, take a moment to acknowledge them and kindly return to the body.
- Know that you can always return to your breath or briefly open your eyes to help ground and settle yourself.
- As you exhale, let go of the pelvis, and as you inhale, shift your attention to feel the whole length of the back. Feel the lower back and the upper back. Perhaps detect sensations of touch where the body meets the chair or the mat.
- Shift your attention to the belly. Feel the sensations in the belly, including the movement of the breath.
- Bring your attention up to the region of the chest. Feel the ribs and muscles as you breathe. Perhaps feel the heartbeat.
- Shift your attention down both arms into the hands. Feel any numbness or moisture in the hands.

- As you exhale, let go of the hands, and as you inhale, shift your attention into both arms. Feel the length of the arms, the skin, and the muscles.
- Shift your attention into the shoulders. Feel any tension or holding, and carefully attend to this region as you breathe.
- Now let go of the shoulders, and shift your attention up to feel the neck and throat. Perhaps feel the breath in the throat or the air on the skin.
- Next, shift your attention up to the face. Feel the face in this moment, noticing any tension or tingling. Simply breathe with the sensations in the whole face.
- Finally, shift your attention to feel the very top of the head. When you are ready, allow your attention to spread slowly down from your head to include the whole body, all the way down to the feet.
- Breathe for a few moments, appreciating your body just as it is.

17. MOVE MINDFULLY

🕐 10 minutes

Movement can be a helpful way to bring our attention into the present moment. Especially when we are feeling stuck or resisting the present moment, bringing movement to the body can allow us to move through difficult emotions. To this day, when I'm feeling overwhelmed, I think of a simple but wise phrase my mom used when I was young: "Move a muscle, change a thought."

- Begin this practice by standing with your knees slightly bent and your feet apart and lined up with your hips.
- Feel the sensations of the body. Maybe shift your weight forward and backward slightly and then come to a place of balance.
- As you stand in stillness, take a moment to acknowledge the intention to get in touch with the sensations of the body as you move. Mind your own limits, and feel free to modify each movement as needed, or even imagine yourself doing the movement if it isn't possible for

(CONTINUED)

you. Feel free to open or close your eyes—whatever helps you stay balanced and in touch with sensations. Notice any judging or striving that arises, and see whether you can gently let it go.

- Start off by reaching the arms up overhead so that both hands point up toward the ceiling. Gaze either forward or up toward your hands, whichever is comfortable for you. Feel the length of the body and the sensations of reaching.
- Slowly, with awareness, lower your arms so they rest alongside your body. Take a moment to feel the effects of this movement in the body.
- Next, reach one arm up overhead, as if picking fruit from a tree, and then reach up with the other. Continue this movement as you breathe, and attend to the sensations it creates in your body.
- With awareness, lower your arms so they rest alongside the body. Take a few breaths to be with the body and whatever sensations arise.
- Next, move your shoulders in gentle circles going forward. After a few moments, reverse directions.
- Slowly, come to stillness. Feel the aftereffects of this movement in the body.
- Bring your right ear toward your right shoulder, and feel the sensations in the neck as you breathe. When you are ready, bring your left ear to your left shoulder. Continue to breathe and attend to the sensations.
- Bring your head back to center, and take a few moments to feel the whole body standing here. Gently hold it all in your awareness.
- As this practice comes to an end, take a moment to become aware of any judgments you might be holding about this practice or your body, and see whether you can gently release them.

18. COUNTING JUDGMENTS IN REAL LIFE

🕐 5 minutes   ✏ pen and paper

When we judge, we often fuel the strong emotions, urges, and behaviors that drive depression. This is especially true when judgments go unnoticed. When I find myself saying, "I shouldn't have to deal with this," I know I'm stuck. When we become aware of judgmental thoughts, they lose some of their power over us. Noticing judgment is the first step to getting unstuck.

- Choose a day to become aware of judgments as they arise. Make sure to have a way to tally the judgments you notice, either on your phone or on a piece of paper.
- As you go through your day, any time you notice a judgmental thought, make a mark on your tally sheet. These thoughts might include words like "good," "bad," "amazing," "terrible," "fair," "unfair," "should," and "shouldn't."
- Especially during times when you start to feel upset or experience a strong emotion, turn your attention inward to notice what you are thinking and whether there are any judgments arising.
- Remember that there is no need to judge yourself for judging. It's a natural part of being alive. Becoming aware of judgments—as opposed to being swept away by them—is the practice of non-judgment.
- Pay particular attention to judgments that arise during transitions in the day, after finishing a conversation or before entering a new activity.
- Count up your tally sheet at the end of the day. Take some time to reflect on the judgments you noticed and how they affected your mood, emotions, and energy.

19. TAKING THE BLINDERS OFF

© 10 minutes

When we are not aware of our thinking, we become our thinking. Being caught in the grip of strong emotions, it is like wearing blinders: We only see what confirms our negative thinking. We are unable to consider the larger picture. The practice of non-judgment is about noticing judgmental thoughts without buying into them. In this exercise, we practice labeling thoughts and noticing any perspective this creates.

- Find a comfortable seated posture. Allow your spine to be straight and relaxed. Let your eyes gently close, or cast your gaze softly downward.
- Begin by attending to the sensations of sitting. Sense any points of touch or contact in the body, and notice the feeling of being grounded, held by the surface you are on.
- Now become aware of the fact that you are breathing. Begin to follow the sensations of inhaling and exhaling wherever you feel them most strongly.
- After a time, you will notice thinking. When this happens, take a moment to notice where the mind has gone, and gently label it. Then gently let go of thinking and come back to following the breath.
- Rather than getting caught up in the content of thoughts, see whether you can bring a sense of curiosity to what you notice.
- If you become aware of a judgment, gently label this thought: "judgmental thought." Use mindfulness to not judge yourself for being judgmental, and gently let go and return to the breath.
- Continue this practice for some time, until you are comfortable following your breath and labeling thoughts and judgments as they arise in the practice.

20. HAVE YOUR OWN BACK

(Mini-Meditation)

As you move through your day, if you become aware of self-criticism or judgment, take a moment to acknowledge these thoughts. With this awareness, consider whether these thoughts are something you would say to a friend or someone you love. See whether this perspective can help you make space for a moment of compassion for yourself. Perhaps even say to yourself, *Ouch, what a harsh thought.*

---

21. FINDING PATTERNS, FREEING THE MIND

🕐 10 minutes   ✐ pen and paper

When we judge something, we create distance between ourselves and the difficult experience. We think, "That sucks," or "They're just rude," or "I just hate it." Underneath the judgment, we frequently find disappointment, hurt, or anger. Judging can feel soothing in the moment, but it's often counterproductive, keeping emotions around even longer. In this MBCT exercise, we get underneath judgment by noticing our reactions to the unpleasantness that often gives rise to patterns of judgment and reactivity.

- Each day for one week, set the intention to become aware of unpleasant experiences as they arise.
- When you notice unpleasantness in the body or mind, pause and investigate it. Take note of the following: What is the situation? What sensations do you notice in your body? What thoughts are present in the mind? What emotions are you experiencing? Are there any urges you feel or actions you feel like taking?

(CONTINUED)

- As soon as you can, write down the answers to each of these questions. As you record and reflect on your experience, write down the thoughts that are currently arising about the experience.
- At the end of the week, take a moment to look over what you recorded and see whether anything stands out. Do you notice any patterns in what comes along with unpleasantness?

22. BACK IN THE DRIVER'S SEAT

It's challenging to keep our thoughts in perspective, especially when we are experiencing strong emotions. Imagine a time when you have been upset and had the thought "I can't do this" or "I just need to get this done." When these thoughts seem like absolute truths, they take the driver's seat. In this meditation, we will notice judgments as they arise and take time to pause, non-judgmentally labeling them as what they are: thoughts. In this way, we can get back in the driver's seat.

- Start by choosing a day when you plan to complete this exercise. At first, try choosing an ordinary day. As time goes on, you might choose a day when you know you will face stress or challenges.
- At the beginning of the day, make sure to set the intention to notice negative thoughts, especially judgments, as they arise.
- Strong emotions or restlessness are good cues that judgments may be around. When you notice a judgment arising, take a moment to notice the thought going through the mind. For example, "I am no good," "I screwed that up," "This isn't fair." Then see whether you can rephrase it to yourself by adding, "I am having the thought that _____."
- There is no need to do anything else. Just notice the judgment and acknowledge that this is a thought that you are having, not an absolute truth.
- Each time you become aware of judgmental thinking or negative self-talk throughout the day, continue this practice.
- When you do this, become aware of any effect this practice has on your sensations and emotions.

- At the end of the day, reflect on what you noticed. If this practice was helpful, see whether you can incorporate it more frequently.

23. CULTIVATING CURIOSITY

© 10 minutes

The judging mind is constantly evaluating our experience or comparing it to some standard we can't seem to meet. In many ways, curiosity is the antidote to the judging mind. It invites us to investigate reality. With this approach, when we notice the thought "I feel terrible," we can ask ourselves, *What is actually here right now? What does terrible feel like? What sensations, emotions, and thoughts am I aware of right now?* Pema Chödrön described this practice when she said, "Drop the story and find the feeling."

- Find a seat that is comfortable, with your body upright and awake to the present moment. Start by taking a few deep breaths to settle.
- Begin to feel the sensations of sitting here. Feel where the body meets the chair or the cushion and where the hands rest on your lap or legs.
- Expand your attention to feel the whole body sitting here.
- If you find your mind is pulled into judging, see whether you can drop the story and find the feeling. Gently let go of thinking, and cultivate curiosity about any sensations or lack of sensations in the body.
- As you breathe, if you become aware of any sensations in the body that call for your attention, feel free to explore them. Bring a sense of curiosity as you carefully investigate their quality and any change or movement.
- If the sensations become too intense, anchor your attention on the breath or on some area of the body that feels neutral or pleasant.
- As this practice ends, take a moment to reconnect with the breath as you re-enter the day.

24. UNPACKING JUDGMENTS

🕐 10 minutes

When we move quickly into our habitual patterns, we never get to know and trust our capacity to be with difficult emotions. With mindfulness, we see that emotions like hurt and disappointment come and go if we let them be. By unpacking judgments and observing the emotions that underlie them, we can move through difficulty with grace.

- Find a quiet place to sit, and adopt a comfortable position. Gently allow your eyes to close, or cast your gaze softly downward.
- Take a few moments to ground yourself in the moment by following the sensations of the breath. Gently feel the movement of the breath in the body.
- When you are ready, bring to mind a judgment that is fresh but not too intense. Let the judgment be present in the mind, and take a moment to observe the "story" or the thoughts that arise.
- Then deliberately let go of thinking, and turn your attention to the feelings in the body. Gently scan your body, and notice whether you can detect any sensations of contraction, tightness, or holding.
- Are there any sensations in your body that come along with this judgment? Carefully and kindly, breathe into and out of the region of greatest intensity. Perhaps as you exhale, you say, *softening, opening*.
- If your mind gets pulled back into the story, gently let go, and notice how the body feels. Kindly investigate the sensations just as they are.
- See whether you detect any emotions, and gently label them. Remember that all of you is welcome. Bring a compassionate and gentle attention to whatever you notice.
- Let go and spend a few moments coming back to feeling your breath. Allow your eyes to open, and take a few deep breaths to release any tension.

25. CLEAR VS. MUDDY EMOTIONS

🕐 10 minutes

Emotions communicate important information about our values and what we care about. This wisdom is often lost when, not wanting to feel pain, we move into fixing or avoiding. In their book *The Mindful Way through Anxiety*, Dr. Susan M. Orsillo and Dr. Lizabeth Roemer make a distinction between "clear" and "muddy" emotions. Clear emotions arise as a direct and often informative response to a situation. An example is feeling hurt in response to being left out. However, we usually spend far more time in guilt or anger, muddy emotions not based on the facts of the situation but on our interpretations, assumptions, or old habits. In this exercise, we practice getting out of the mud.

- Take a moment to sit quietly, with your spine straight and relaxed. Take a few deep breaths.
- Bring to mind a situation where you feel stuck, perhaps one that you have a lot of judgment about. Simply describe what occurred (e.g., my friend did not invite me to dinner).
- Consider the story that you are telling yourself about the situation (e.g., they are a bad friend). Notice how it affects you in body and mind. Notice how adhesive the story is.
- Now let go of the story and allow thinking to fade into the background. Consider all of the emotions that are present. Then, one by one, try to label them.
- Reflect on the emotions that are a direct response to the situation you identified. These are your clear emotions.
- Now notice which emotions come from your interpretations, predictions, or past experiences. Feel the extra layer of suffering these emotions create. These are your muddy emotions. Invite an attitude of beginner's mind, and remember that we don't know the future and can't read others' minds.

(CONTINUED)

- Finally, go back to the clear emotions and take a few moments to sit and breathe. As you breathe, consider what these clear emotions might be telling you or asking of you. Continue to breathe, and open up to any clarity or ease that arises.

26. TOP 10 GREATEST HITS

🕐 10 minutes   ✏ pen and paper

As we spend time watching our mind, we may notice that certain thoughts feel familiar, like they are on constant rotation when things are not going well. Some thoughts arise from past experiences—things others said to us or we grew up hearing. Others are reflections of universal symptoms of depression. Wherever they come from, one thing is certain: These depression-related thoughts can easily take hold and drag us down, making it hard to take mindful action. In this exercise, we name these self-defeating thoughts our "Top 10 Greatest Hits." In this way, we can learn to see these habits of the mind more clearly.

- Find a place where you can have some privacy. You will need a paper and pen.
- Before you start writing, take a few moments to ground yourself in the moment. Sit with your eyes closed and feel the body breathing. When you feel settled, allow your eyes to open.
- Take a few moments to reflect on the patterns of thinking you have noticed so far. What self-defeating thoughts tend to arise in meditation and in daily life?
- Consider your "greatest hits"—the thoughts that appear again and again. Write them down.
- After you complete your list, spend a moment writing yourself a short note or encouraging reminder to help you maintain a compassionate perspective when you notice a hit come along.
- See whether when these thoughts arise, you can gently note, *Ah, there is one of my greatest hits*. Bring a kind and patient awareness to the thought, and let it go.

27. LOVING-KINDNESS

🕐 10 minutes

It's hard to practice non-judgment of others when we are busy judging ourselves. We can work to counteract the judging mind by purposefully cultivating warmth and care toward others and ourselves. Loving-kindness, a practice adopted from Buddhism, is intended to loosen the layers of judgment and reactivity to let our true loving nature shine through more brightly.

- Sit in a comfortable posture, and gently allow your eyes to close. Start by sensing yourself seated here in this moment. Allow the sensations of the body and the breath to ground you in this moment.
- Once you feel settled, bring to mind someone you love and care for deeply. This someone can be an animal, a child, a trusted mentor, or a friend.
- With this person in mind, begin to sense your true wish for them to be well. As you do this, offer these phases silently to your person:

    May you be happy

    May you be healthy

    May you be peaceful

    May you be loved

- Continue to repeat the phrases for a few minutes, and direct them toward your person as you breathe. When your mind wanders, see whether you can gently let go and return to sending these kind wishes.
- If you are comfortable, place your hand on your chest or body as you breathe, feeling the warmth you are creating.

(CONTINUED)

- Next, acknowledge your own desire to be happy, healthy, peaceful, and loved. Begin to take this loving-kindness you have cultivated and direct it toward yourself.

  May I be happy

  May I be healthy

  May I be peaceful

  May I be loved

- Continue to repeat the phrases for a few minutes and direct them toward yourself as you breathe. Let the intention to cultivate loving-kindness toward yourself be enough.
- As you complete this practice, take a moment to let go of these phrases and simply feel any sensations or emotions that are present.

28. AN ATTITUDE OF INNER FRIENDLINESS

🕐 10 minutes

Self-compassion forms an attitude of inner friendliness that can go a long way toward short-circuiting old patterns of harshness and criticism. Self-compassion means that in times of struggle, we bring awareness to reality and attempt to treat ourselves with the same kindness and understanding that we would offer a dear friend. At a deep level, this means recognizing that we all struggle and feel pain. In this practice, we learn how to counter self-judgment with self-compassion.

- Sit in an upright and comfortable position. Allow your eyes to gently close, or cast your gaze softly on the floor.
- Take a few deep breaths to ground yourself in this moment.
- Gently place a hand over your heart and feel the movement of the breath. See whether you can allow your heart to be soft and receptive.

- Once you feel settled with the breath, allow the following questions to drop into your awareness: *What do I need? What is my intention for practicing mindfulness?*
- Take a moment to let this question settle. Allow the answer to be a universal need: peace, freedom, ease, love, connection. Acknowledge whatever arises for you, and hold it in your heart.
- Repeat this need as a kind wish for yourself: *May I be_____.*
- Continue to breathe with your hand on your heart as you repeat this phrase to yourself. Feel the realness of this wish for yourself. Sit and breathe with any sensations or emotions this creates.
- As this practice ends, write down your phrase, and use it in meditation or any time you feel self-judgment arise.

29. NON-JUDGMENTAL COMMUNICATION

Practicing non-judgment enriches our interactions with others. When we pass judgment on those we do not know, we shut ourselves off from them without understanding. When we pass judgment on those we know, we create distance and tension. Judgment only fuels isolation and loneliness. By practicing non-judgment in our communication with others, we can build a bridge so that we no longer feel separate. Try this practice to build a bridge in your interactions.

- Choose an interaction where you plan to practice non-judgmental communication.
- Begin by using mindfulness to become aware of when judgments arise. When you **notice** judgmental thinking, you are not **being** judgmental.
- See whether you can bring a sense of curiosity to the interaction by asking questions. Genuinely attempt to understand. Reflect on what might be going on with this person and what might be affecting their viewpoint or behavior.

(CONTINUED)

- Notice any thoughts, emotions, or sensations in your body. Kindly acknowledge your response. Give yourself and the other person permission to have your own unique ideas and feelings. Accept that we are all different.
- Approaching communication in this way is an act of bravery and kindness. If you are able, perhaps take a moment to consider this kindness. What changes arise when you approach communication in this way? Are there any downsides to bringing curiosity instead of judgment? What have you learned?

Words of Encouragement

Simply becoming more aware of judgment and how it affects our experience us is a huge step forward. We are not trying to get rid of judging altogether. With mindfulness practice, we work more wisely with judgment when it arises. Freed from fusion and reactivity, we can harness our intelligence and energy to be guided by our values and compassion for ourselves and others.

Reflection

What did you notice as you worked through these meditations? What aspects of your experience stood out? How can you apply the attitude of non-judgment to your daily life?

Mindfulness Meditations for Depression

Clearly recognizing what is happening inside us, and regarding what we see with an open, kind and loving heart, is what I call Radical Acceptance. If we are holding back from any part of our experience, if our heart shuts out any part of who we are and what we feel, we are fueling the fears and feelings of separation that sustain the trance of unworthiness.

—Tara Brach, psychologist and author

CHAPTER FOUR

Acceptance

We all struggle with acceptance. We want things to be a certain way. Much of this struggle can be understood in terms of our habitual patterns of attachment and aversion.

Attachment is our tendency to cling to what feels good. When something pleasant happens, we want more of it. We wish to feel better and when we finally do, we start to worry about how long it will last.

Aversion is the tendency to resist difficult experiences. When something unpleasant happens, we want to change or get rid of it. When we experience depression, these patterns of clinging and resisting intensify our distress as we are faced with highs and lows that are sometimes out of our control. These patterns bring us to the central concept of this chapter: how to hold space for what is.

53

Acceptance is a choice to be with the truth of the moment. This means letting go of how we wish things were or what we deem is "right." With mindfulness, we can begin to become aware of attachment and aversion and how they add to our suffering. If we think of suffering as the combination of pain and resistance, the goal is not to remove pain but to examine our resistance. How we respond to difficulty can either fuel it or allow it to burn out on its own.

As we practice acceptance, we come to see that letting go is quite the opposite of losing or giving up. It can help us find steadiness in the face of life's unavoidable ups and downs. When we stop fighting or clinging, we create resources we didn't know we had for self-care and flourishing.

Common Unhelpful Thoughts

> *This can't be happening again.*
> *I can't handle this.*
> *I don't want it to be this way.*

30. SOFTENING

🕐 5 minutes

Very often, non-acceptance is our way of protecting ourselves from unwanted pain, disappointment, or hurt. In this self-protective state, we become rigid as we physically harden and brace against reality. Learning to soften our body can be a doorway to soften our responses as we learn to meet the moment with greater receptivity and flexibility.

- To begin this meditation, find a seat that allows the body to be relaxed yet awake. Perhaps shift to each side until you find a place of balance, and let your eyes close.
- As you settle in, take a few deeper breaths before allowing the breath to settle into its natural rhythm.

- Now begin to attend to the sensations in the face, mouth, and jaw. If you notice any obvious tightness or holding, gently allow this to soften. Perhaps allow the tongue to fall away from the roof of your mouth, letting the jaw relax.
- Tune into the sensations in the shoulders. Allow them to gently relax down the back. As you exhale, see whether you can allow any tension to melt away.
- Begin to attend to sensations in the hands. If you notice any gripping or stiffness, gently invite it to loosen as you exhale. Let the hands soften.
- Finally, tune into the belly and see whether you can let your belly be soft. Gently let go of any holding or tightness in your belly, and allow your belly to relax.
- For the last few moments of this practice, tune into the sensations of the whole body sitting here. Allow the body to be held in a kind and spacious awareness, open to whatever arises.

31. TWO FEET, ONE BREATH
(Mini-Meditation)

As you transition between physical spaces throughout the day, be sure to pause and feel your feet on the ground. Be aware of one full cycle of your breath before proceeding mindfully. Try this any time you move from room to room, like entering a meeting or coming home at the end of the day. Let this practice help you meet the next moments of your day with openness and acceptance.

32. POWER IN THE SPACE BETWEEN

🕐 10 minutes

Acceptance allows us to see our typical patterns of reactivity with a bit more space between thoughts, emotions, urges, and actions. This space and the freedom of choice that it brings profoundly affects our actions and our lives. In this way, acceptance and allowing actually give us back control, not over our thoughts or emotions, but over our actions. We nurture this ability by recognizing and then choosing to welcome all experiences—pleasant, unpleasant, and neutral—with the same essential friendliness.

- Find a relaxed and comfortable posture. You can allow your eyes to close or cast your gaze softly on the floor.
- Take a moment to acknowledge the intention of this practice: to recognize your experience, however it is, with a sense of allowing and even welcoming. Remember, there is nothing to do or achieve for the next few minutes aside from noticing whatever arises.
- Take a few deep breaths, and let your attention settle wherever you feel your breath most clearly. Spend a few minutes following the sensations of the inhale and exhale. Allow the breath to simply come and go.
- As you breathe, you may become aware of moments of ease or focus and moments of agitation and struggle. See whether you can meet each of these moments with the same kind awareness. Perhaps label experiences as they arise: *Ah, agitation is here.* Then gently guide your attention back to the breath.
- Now shift your attention from the breath to feel the whole body breathing. Spend a few minutes carefully observing sensations in the body just as they are. Feel them shift, change, and stay the same.
- As you attend to the sensations of the body, you may become aware of sensations of lightness or warmth or tightness and pain. See whether you can meet each of these sensations with the same friendly

awareness. Perhaps label experiences as they arise: *Ah, tension is here.* Then gently guide your attention back to your body.

- As this practice comes to an end, take a few moments to feel the breath once more. See whether you can acknowledge your efforts to build this space of acceptance and allowing in your life.

33. RECEIVING SOUND FROM ALL AROUND

🕐 5 minutes

Acceptance allows us to work wisely with the resistance that often comes with change. Our lives are always in flux, very often due to forces outside of our control. Making peace with this truth is a key to our survival—as the Zen proverb tells us, "Let go or be dragged." As we learn to accept, everyday experience can be our teacher. This exercise helps us practice simply being with the changing flow of sounds, fostering an attitude of acceptance in the face of life's noise.

- Find a comfortable seat in a noisy area, perhaps in a park or on public transportation. Allow your spine to be straight, and let your gaze be soft. Let your shoulders and belly gently relax.
- For a few moments, focus on the sensations of the breath.
- After a time, let the breath fade into the background, and shift your attention to sounds. Open up to hearing what is around you.
- If you become aware that sounds lead to thoughts or emotions, see whether you can acknowledge that and gently let go and return to hearing. See whether you can accept sounds from all around.
- Notice how sounds simply rise and fall. With a sense of curiosity and patience, rest in the moment and listen. Simply experience sounds without thinking about them or trying to control them.

(CONTINUED)

- Notice sounds that are close by and far away. Notice sounds from inside the body and outside the body. See whether you can rest with an open and accepting stance, welcoming whatever comes.
- For the last few moments of this practice, allow sounds to fade into the background and feel the sensations of the breath.
- See whether you can bring this sense of openness to the next moments of your day.

---

34. WALK IN PEACE

○ 10 minutes

Mindful walking encourages us to embody acceptance. Although we are moving, the purpose is not to arrive anywhere in particular. With each step, there is no goal but to be with what is. Thich Nhat Hanh describes this powerful practice: "The mind can go in a thousand directions. But on this beautiful path, I walk in peace. With each step, a gentle wind blows. With each step, a flower blooms."

- Choose a place where you have about ten to thirty paces to walk back and forth. You can choose a place inside or outside, depending on your preference. If you need accommodations for your mobility, feel free to adapt the movement part of this meditation to fit your needs. The point is to move with intention and attention, however it is that you move through the world.
- Start by standing still, feeling the weight of the body. Let the shoulders relax, and allow the arms to rest in a position that is comfortable for you.
- As you begin to walk, move far more slowly than you normally would. Move with intention, and feel the microsensations in the feet and legs as you shift your weight onto one foot, slowly lift the other foot, move it forward, and place it down.
- Allow the sensations of walking to be an anchor for your attention. Whenever the mind wanders, gently guide it back to feeling the feet and to walking. Whether the mind has been gone for just a minute or

quite a while, it's okay. Each time, simply come back to the experience of walking.

- When you arrive at the end of the path, pause for a moment to feel the sensations in the body. Then slowly turn to face the other direction. Pause for a moment to gather your attention, then begin walking again.
- As you walk, if you become aware of any strong experiences, pause and take a moment to welcome them with a gentle heart. Gently let go and resume walking.
- Finally, take a moment to appreciate your effort to move mindfully and consider how you can integrate it into your daily life.

35. RIDING THE WAVES

○ 10 minutes

Just as we cannot stop the waves of the ocean with our efforts, thoughts will continually arise, one after another. Acceptance allows us to navigate these waves of thought with greater ease. The practice of acknowledging and allowing thoughts saves us from fighting the waves or being pulled into the current. When we meet thoughts with awareness and acceptance, we stop the struggle. We can take the advice of meditation teacher and author Eckhart Tolle: "Whatever the present moment contains, accept it as if you had chosen it. Always work with it, not against it."

- Find a comfortable and dignified posture. Allow your eyes to gently close, or cast your gaze softly in front of you. Let the hands rest easily on your lap or legs.
- Take a few moments to settle yourself by attending to the sensations of the breath.

(CONTINUED)

- Now allow the breath to fade into the background, and begin to become aware of thoughts. Rather than being carried away by the content of thoughts, see whether you can recognize when thinking is happening. Simply note thoughts passing through the mind.
- You may like to imagine thoughts as waves crashing one by one onto the shore. Some are heavy and pass quite slowly. Others are light and move quickly across the sand. Whatever their content, kindly note each one.
- Some thoughts might bring with them an emotional charge, and if so, note that, too.
- If you become caught up in the storyline of your thoughts, see whether you can gently let go and return to observing. Accept all that arises with an attitude of patience and gentleness.
- As you work with thinking in this way, thoughts and emotions become less personal, more like waves in the spacious ocean.

36. RUMI'S GUEST HOUSE

🕐 5 minutes

Below is a poem by Rumi, a thirteenth-century poet, scholar, and Muslim theologian. Read this poem twice and follow the instructions on the next page.

> *This being human is a guest house.*
> *Every morning a new arrival.*
>
> *A joy, a depression, a meanness,*
> *some momentary awareness comes*
> *as an unexpected visitor.*

Welcome and entertain them all!
Even if they're a crowd of sorrows,
who violently sweep your house
empty of its furniture,
still, treat each guest honorably.
He may be clearing you out
for some new delight.

The dark thought, the shame, the malice,
meet them at the door laughing,
and invite them in.

Be grateful for whoever comes,
because each has been sent
as a guide from beyond.

- Sit quietly and feel the breath. Allow any thoughts, emotions, or sensations in your body to be fully acknowledged and felt.
- Take a moment to reflect on this poem and how it invites us to meet our own experiences. Are there certain guests that you reject? Do they truly go away when we close the door? What are the effects of saying "no" to unwanted guests? What might be helpful about taking a more welcoming stance? Observe any tension or bracing that arises at the idea of being more welcoming. Consider any times when difficult experiences have brought about growth or strength.
- Let go of thinking, and allow your attention to rest on the sensations of the breath. Let whatever has been stirred up start to settle as you rest in stillness.
- Experiment with an attitude of acceptance as you encounter visitors during your day.

37. HALF SMILE

🕐 5 minutes

We can often detect non-acceptance as tension, bracing, or clenching in our body. At the same time, our body feeds back and communicates with our brain, affecting our thoughts and emotions. Because of this interaction, working directly on our body can have a profound effect on how we think and feel. In this practice, we use a half smile to help cultivate an attitude of acceptance.

- Begin by finding a seat that feels comfortable, with your spine straight and also relaxed. Let your hands rest gently in your lap, and allow your eyes to softly close.
- Begin to attend to the sensations of the breath wherever you feel them most clearly. Carefully follow the sensations of the breath as you allow the body to simply breathe.
- If you become aware that your attention is no longer on the breath, gently guide it back, without judgment or criticism.
- Next, bring a gentle half smile to the mouth. Allow your face to relax, and invite the sides of the mouth to turn slightly upward.
- Let the eyes be soft, and continue to breathe with a gentle half smile on the lips.
- As you breathe with this half smile, allow your awareness to expand to the entire body. Notice any sensations that arise in the body.
- As this practice comes to an end, know that you can return to this half smile to foster acceptance and ease.

38. SWITCHING GEARS

🕐 3 minutes

Another way to promote acceptance is to move from the "doing mind" to the "being mind." We use the "doing mind" to accomplish tasks and solve problems in our external world, but when we apply the "doing mind" to our internal experience, it often breaks down, and we tend to feel worse. The "being mind" is about being present with our experiences, even painful ones, rather than automatically being pulled to do something about them. This mode of mind promotes acceptance and can counteract rumination, self-blame, and reactivity. In MBCT, the three-minute breathing space is used as a way to become aware of our mind mode and switch gears. Try using this practice several times a day at regular intervals, and see what you notice. You will see other versions of the three-minute breathing space later in this book.

- Begin by adopting a posture that is upright and awake, and allow this posture to signal coming into the present moment.
- In step one of the breathing space, take a minute to **turn your attention inward**, noticing your experience in this moment.
- Scan the body and notice any sensations. Become aware of how the body feels, without striving to change anything. Notice any emotions that arise. See whether you notice any thoughts passing through the mind. Without pushing away any thoughts or elaborating on them, gently label each one: "thought about the future," "thought about the past," and so on. Once you have taken stock of your experience, perhaps say to yourself, *Okay, this is how it is right now.*
- In step two of the breathing space, take a minute to **focus on your breath**. Feel the sensations of the breath coming in and out. Let other experiences fade into the background.

(CONTINUED)

- In step three of the breathing space, take a minute to **expand your attention** to the whole body. Breathe with a sense of the body and any sensations or experiences that arise.
- See whether you can maintain an open and spacious awareness, bringing this awareness throughout your day.

39. SAYING YES

🕐 10 minutes

Unwillingness to be with difficult thoughts, emotions, or sensations can be a trigger for patterns of self-judgment that leave us vulnerable to further escalation. Acceptance can short-circuit these old patterns and allow us to form new ones. In her book *Radical Acceptance*, Tara Brach describes this practice as saying "yes" to the moment. She says, "There is something wonderfully bold and liberating about saying yes to our entire imperfect and messy life." In this exercise, we practice doing just that.

- Begin this meditation by taking a comfortable seat. Allow your spine to be straight and relaxed. Your eyes can gently close, or you can cast your gaze softly in front of you.
- Tune in to the sensations of the breath. Feel the breath at your nostrils, chest, or belly, wherever it feels clearest to you.
- Gently follow the length of the inhale and the length of the exhale.
- As you become aware of other experiences, see whether you can practice saying "yes"—to the critical thought, the numbness in the foot, even the feeling of anxiety in the chest. Once you have acknowledged the experience, take a moment to observe it and let it go, returning to the breath.
- Even if this feels artificial at first, see whether you can bring a sense of openness and acceptance to all experiences as they present themselves.
- Continue to breathe, and any time your attention is drawn away, kindly and gently note the experience and say "yes."

- As this practice comes to an end, take a moment to reflect on this practice of saying "yes." Know that saying "yes" doesn't mean that you have to like it. It simply means you are choosing to acknowledge things just as they are before deciding whether and how to respond.

40. EXPLORING DIFFICULTY

🕐 10 minutes

As we watch closely, we begin to see that many old patterns come from a place of self-protection. At one point, they served us. Still, with the recognition that our old strategies of avoidance and suppression no longer work, we can begin to experiment with a new way of being with difficulty. To shift to a new pattern takes practice. The following exercise can help us begin to work with situations that are hard to accept by exploring the difficulty rather than rejecting it. Perhaps there is a conflict or annoyance that keeps coming back to you? Focus on that as you work through this exercise.

- At a time when you are not acutely upset, find a comfortable seat where you feel alert and awake.
- Take a few moments to feel the body grounded, sitting here in this moment. Notice points of contact where the body meets the surface you are sitting on.
- Begin to shift your attention to the sensations of the breath. Feel the whole length of the inhale and the whole length of the exhale. Follow the breath until you feel settled.
- Bring to mind a situation that is bothering you, one that feels hard to accept. Acknowledge the facts of the situation and allow it to be there for a moment.
- Shift your attention to the body and begin to gently scan to see whether you can detect any sensations of holding, tension, or tightness.

(CONTINUED)

- Spend some time breathing with the sensations you notice. Send breath into and out from the region of greatest intensity. As a gesture of acceptance and allowing, perhaps say, *It's okay. It's already here. Let me be with this.*
- See whether you can stay with the feelings in the body, as opposed to getting pulled back into the story in the mind. As you breathe in and out of any sensations you find, repeat the words *softening, opening* as you breathe out. (This is not meant to change anything but to help you be more present with your difficulty.)
- After a time, let go of the difficulty and guide your attention back to the breath. Allow the breath to anchor you in the moment. Carefully follow the sensations as the body breathes in and breathes out.
- As this practice comes to an end, congratulate yourself for your willingness to be with difficulty in this way.

41. MOUNTAIN MEDITATION

◷ 10 minutes

Acceptance offers us the possibility of seeing the dark cloud of depression—the fatigue, loss of interest, and sadness—with less reactivity. In the thick of the storm, acceptance helps us see that despite our predictions, the weather will change, and the storm will pass. The mountain has much to teach us about weathering storms with steadiness and equanimity. Try this practice when you are feeling relatively settled. Eventually, you may harness it in times of tumult.

- Start by sitting in an upright and dignified position. If you are able, sit on the floor with your legs crossed underneath you, or on a chair.
- Spend some time feeling the body grounded here. Notice points of contact or pressure where the body is held by the earth. Also feel the body lifting upward as you sit.
- Notice any areas of tension, and let go to the degree you can. Take a few deep breaths to settle yourself in the moment, and allow thoughts and worries from the day to fade into the background.

- Bring to mind the image of a mountain. This can be a mountain you have seen or one you imagine. Take a few moments to see this mountain—the base where it meets the ground and the peak as it rises up. Observe how massive, unmoving, and majestic it is.
- When you feel ready, see whether you can bring the mountain into your own body, so your body is the mountain. You are the mountain, sharing the same greatness and stillness.
- As you sit here, become aware of how day after day the sun rises and sets on the mountain. As day becomes night and night becomes day, the mountain remains steady and calm.
- In summer, the sun beats down on your mountain body, hot and dry. In fall, the mountain wears brilliant colors in the leaves of the trees. In winter, the mountain is covered with snow or drenched by freezing rain. In spring, new life slowly emerges. In each season, the mountain remains unchanged at its core.
- Perhaps people come to see the mountain. Some comment on how imposing and beautiful it is; others are unmoved by its majesty. Note how the mountain's presence and splendor are unaffected by the way people see it.
- In meditation, we can experience and learn from the mountain. We come to embody the same sense of unwavering stillness. Just like the mountain, our inner and outer experiences are constantly changing. We have our own periods of light and dark, stormy weather and calm skies.
- As this practice ends, take a moment to consider how we can learn to work wisely with the weather of our own lives. Perhaps we can learn to take the changing weather of our experience less personally, seeing its ever-changing nature, and perhaps touching into a deep stillness, quiet, and wisdom.

42. SELF-ACCEPTANCE

🕐 10 minutes

Sometimes we get stuck in a cycle of striving, comparing, or trying to problem-solve our present reality. We become preoccupied with how we can be better or more successful. With self-acceptance, we can learn to start from a place of wholeness rather than deficiency. As the psychologist Carl Rogers said, "The curious paradox is that when I accept myself as I am, then I change."

- Find a position where you feel comfortable and at ease. Feel the sensations of sitting here.
- Take a few deep breaths to help you arrive in this moment. Then allow the breath to return to its natural rhythm. Let the breath anchor you in the present.
- When you feel settled, bring to mind some aspect of your personality you fault yourself for or some mistake that you have judged yourself harshly for lately. Take a moment to allow this perceived inadequacy to settle in the mind. Notice any emotions that arise. Perhaps name the emotions.
- See whether you can locate these emotions anywhere in the body. Scan the body for any sensations of heaviness in the chest, tightness in the throat, or tensing of the jaw. Simply allow these feelings to be here rather than fighting them.
- Notice how much suffering comes with judging. Allow yourself to be moved by how difficult this experience is.
- In a gesture of tenderness, place your hand on your heart or anywhere that brings you comfort.
- When you are ready, begin to repeat the following phrases to yourself:

  May I be peaceful

  May I be kind to myself

  May I accept myself as I am

- Continue to repeat these phrases as you breathe. Know we are all flawed.
- As you end this practice and continue with your day, return to these phrases to reconnect with the intention of self-acceptance.

---

43. JUST THIS ONE BREATH

🕐 5 minutes

In the face of painful situations, acceptance can seem daunting. Accepting a situation that seems wrong may feel like we are giving in. In reality, acceptance is simply saying, *This is how it is right now.* The key phrase is "right now." Acceptance can only happen in each moment. When struggling with acceptance, our breath can serve as our guide. We can focus on getting through just one breath, and then another.

- Sit in a way that feels steady and alert. Allow your shoulders to gently relax down your back, and let your chest be open.
- Take a few deep breaths, and notice where you feel the breath most clearly. Allow your attention to settle there, carefully feeling the sensations as the body inhales and exhales.
- Whenever you become aware that your attention is no longer on the breath, simply notice where your mind has gone, let go, and return to the next breath.
- As you breathe, begin to repeat *just this* on the inhale and *one breath* on the exhale.
- Continue repeating this to yourself as you breathe for several minutes. Bring your full attention to each inhale and each exhale.
- For the last few moments of this practice, let go of this phrase, and just rest with the sensations of the breath.

(CONTINUED)

- As you continue to practice this in meditation, try bringing this phrase into your day when you are having trouble being in the moment. Take one or two breaths to repeat this phrase as a way to turn toward acceptance, then return to your day.

44. HALF SMILE IN DIFFICULT SITUATIONS

🕐 5 minutes

Once you have practiced the half smile in meditation, you can begin to bring it into difficult situations. When you start to detect resistance in yourself, gently bring a half smile to your face, and feel your breath as you do so. You can practice in any interaction, as a way to listen more fully and with openness. An accepting posture in your body can help create this same attitude in your mind. Remember, the half smile can be very subtle, even undetectable to others.

- Choose a situation that you anticipate being difficult, when judgment and non-acceptance may arise. Set the intention to practice using a half smile to cultivate acceptance.
- Notice when difficulty starts to arise in the body or mind. Perhaps you become aware of negative thoughts or tension in the body.
- Gently label whatever is present. Perhaps it is "judgmental thoughts," "irritation," "tightness in the stomach."
- Bring a half smile to your face. Allow the muscles of the face to relax, and allow the corners of the mouth to turn up slightly. If you are having an in-person interaction, this can be a very subtle softening of the face.
- Use the breath as an anchor as you continue to adopt your half smile. Notice any feelings that arise with a sense of opening and allowing.
- As you complete this exercise, take a moment to reflect on how this practice affected your ability to let it be.

Words of Encouragement

Acceptance is not a one-and-done kind of deal. Sometimes, we accept something in one moment, and need to accept it again in the next. Acceptance is a path from which we veer and return. We are on a continual journey of accepting our lives as they are.

Reflection

What did you notice as you worked through these meditations? What aspects of your experience stood out? How can you apply the attitude of acceptance to your daily life?

Mindfulness Meditations for Depression

Try to be mindful, and let things take their natural course. Then your mind will become still in any surroundings, like a clear forest pool.

—Ajahn Chah, Thai Buddhist monk and meditation teacher

CHAPTER FIVE

Patience

Patience is not easy to maintain. We have become accustomed to instant gratification. It often doesn't feel natural to let things unfold in their own time.

The illusion that we should always feel good creates an urgent focus on fixing things. Impatience with discomfort often drives us to attempt to control our environment, ultimately depleting us. The habitual ways we meet discomfort, sadness, or uncertainty by "doing" may provide temporary relief, but in the long term, they intensify our distress and perpetuate suffering if we do not also address the root pain. Sadly, we are so consumed with feeling better that we lose touch with anything our emotions may be offering us about how to get to a peaceful place.

Patience is a form of wisdom. When we tap into this state, we can drop the sense of urgency, settle in, and trust the natural unfolding of our experience. It is helpful to know that when it comes to our difficult thoughts, emotions, and sensations, despite what the thinking mind tells us, nothing lasts forever. In her book *When Things Fall Apart: Heart Advice for Difficult Times*, Pema Chödrön comments on how awareness and patience can help us see how we add to our pain and confusion. She says, "It's a transformative experience to simply pause instead of immediately filling up the space. By waiting, we begin to connect with fundamental restlessness as well as fundamental spaciousness."

Common Unhelpful Thoughts

> *I can't live like this forever.*
> *Something has to change.*
> *My life is not going the way I want it to.*

45. WAVES OF BREATH

🕐 10 minutes

Our breath can be a great teacher of patience. We can settle in and watch it rise and fall like the waves of the ocean. Nothing to do but watch and wait. Yet, the movement of our mind pushes us forward. We get lost in thought, come back to our breath, and get lost once again. Each experience can teach us patience. As meditation teacher Sharon Salzberg advises, "If you have to let go of distractions and begin again thousands of times, fine. That's not a roadblock to the practice—that *is* the practice."

- Begin by sitting in an upright and relaxed position. Allow your eyes to gently close, or cast your gaze softly downward.
- Take a few moments to feel the whole body sitting here. Bring a kind awareness to the body as it is.

- Shift your attention to the sensations of the breath at the belly. Kindly wait and feel the gentle rise and fall of the belly. There is no need to change or control the breath.
- Each time you become aware that your attention is no longer on the breath, gently take note of where it has gone. Maybe label where it went—*ah, sounds* or *ah, remembering.* Then very gently guide your attention back to the breath.
- Shift your attention to the sensations of the breath at the chest. Allow your attention to reside here as you feel the chest rise and fall. Follow the full length of the inhale, perhaps noticing a short pause before the body exhales, and a short pause before the body inhales.
- When you become aware of the mind wandering, see whether you can bring a sense of kindness and patience to the process of noticing and coming back.
- Finally, begin to detect the sensations of the breath at the nostrils. Feel the cool air come in and the warm air go out. Whether the sensations are subtle or strong, bring careful attention as you await each breath.
- For the last few moments of this meditation, feel the full length of the breath in the body, from your belly up to your nose. Allow it to come and go like the waves of the ocean.

46. A MINDFUL MEAL

🕐 20 minutes

In our rush to get on to the next thing or to feel better, we rarely take time to really experience eating. As much as we know that slowing down may help us enjoy our food, feel more satisfied, and take care of our bodies, in the busyness of our lives, we often don't have the patience for it. Practicing mindful eating can help us bring awareness to any sense of urgency or stress so we can enjoy a mindful meal.

(CONTINUED)

- Choose a meal that you might normally eat mindlessly, quickly, and without awareness. It can be helpful to do this alone at first, and then bring this awareness to meals you eat with others.
- Find a quiet place to sit with your food on the table in front of you.
- Take a moment to check in with your hunger level. Notice the sensations in the stomach. Take a few deep breaths to bring yourself into the present.
- Now, take a moment to look at the food in front of you. Examine it carefully with your eyes. Really see it.
- Slowly, with awareness, reach for your food and pick it up. Take a moment to smell it before slowly biting down. Allow yourself time to slowly chew and taste the food. Notice how the taste and texture changes over time. See whether you can put down your food or utensil between bites.
- As you eat, bring your full awareness to the senses involved in each step of the process. Take the time to see, taste, and smell the food as you eat.
- When you become aware that you have shifted out of awareness and back into autopilot, gently let go and guide your attention back to eating, to fully experiencing and appreciating your meal.
- From time to time, check in on your level of hunger. Perhaps take time to have a sip of water.
- Once you have finished eating, take a few moments to sit quietly and feel the body and the breath before continuing on with your day.

47. SLOWING THE PACE

We often don't get to dictate the pace of things. Impatient for the rain to pass or our luck to change, we suffer. Some things simply cannot be rushed. Learning to work with the difficulty of this truth involves patience. When we bravely acknowledge the limits of our control and allow things to unfold in their own time, we can learn to feel at home even with discomfort. In this exercise, we engage in the physical practice of slowing down, inviting the mind to follow.

- Choose a time when you can go for a walk of a known distance. Perhaps walking around the block, to the park, or to the mailbox. Choose somewhere that feels safe and where you can move comfortably. The point is to move with intention and attention, however it is that you move through the world, so feel free to adapt this exercise according to your own mobility needs.
- Start by standing and feeling the sensations in the feet, the legs, and the whole body. Know what it feels like to stand here in this moment. Allow the body to relax to the degree that it will.
- Begin to walk at your natural pace, tuning in to how the movements feel in the body. Bring your full awareness to the sensations of walking.
- If you become distracted from the sensations of walking, take note of where the mind has gone and gently bring it back.
- When you are about one-third of the way through your walk, begin to slow your pace slightly. Allow your movements to become more deliberate, and observe the sensations as you take each step. Feel the muscles engage and the pressure shift from foot to foot.
- If you notice any sense of urgency or impatience, acknowledge it and let go. Each time this happens, return your awareness to walking.
- When you are two-thirds of the way through your walk, see whether you can slow down your pace even more. The pace should feel much slower than normal. As you move, bring careful attention to how it feels as you lift, move, and place each foot on the ground. Continue in this way until the end of your walk.
- Once you have reached the end of your walk, take another moment to stand still, feeling the sensations in the whole body. Consider what arose as you slowed down your pace.

48. WORKING WITH WAITING

In our doing mind, we often become impatient with our circumstances and with ourselves. Needing things to be different or move more quickly, we lose touch with the richness of the moment. We may see everything as an obstacle. The line at the store, the email not returned right away, the old couple slowly crossing the street—all turn into nuisances as opposed to opportunities to pause and wake up to the present moment.

- For this exercise, choose a day or a situation when you intend to practice waiting.
- See whether you can become aware of waiting, and notice if impatience arises. Maybe this is waiting for the bathroom, the elevator, an appointment, a text message, or the light to turn green.
- Stop and take a moment to bring a sense of curiosity to what impatience feels like, without needing to change it. Feel the body, noticing any tension. See whether you can detect what emotions are present. Gently take note of the thoughts that arise in the mind.
- Now shift your attention to feel the weight of the feet on the ground or in your shoes. Notice any other places where the body is grounded—maybe your buttocks on the chair or your hands on the steering wheel or in your lap.
- Tune in to the sensations of the breath. Let the breath ground you in this moment. Allow your doing mind to fade into the background, and feel the breath, moment by moment.
- As this practice comes to an end, allow awareness of the breath to remain in the background as you begin to slowly return to your day.

49. BEING WITH THE BODY

🕐 15 minutes

The body scan is an important practice for cultivating patience. This one is pretty long, which gives the mind lots of time to wander off to questioning what the heck the point of this practice is (*ah, impatience*). Furthermore, sustaining compassionate attention for our sensations—even uncomfortable ones—goes against our tendency to want to change the difficult, hold on to the pleasant, and tune out the neutral. But it's in patience that we eventually find ease.

- Start by finding a comfortable posture, sitting, standing, or lying down. Allow yourself cushions or any other props to make yourself more comfortable. Close your eyes or maintain a soft gaze.
- Take a moment to acknowledge the intention of the body scan: to carefully investigate the sensations in each area of the body. Rather than think about the sensations, see whether you can feel them. As you move through the scan, if there are no sensations in a particular region of the body, that's okay; just rest your attention on that area.
- Begin by feeling your breath in the belly. Follow the inhale and exhale, and allow yourself to arrive in this moment.
- Shift your attention to the feet. Carefully investigate the sensations in the feet. Maybe feel the toes, the arch of the foot, and the heels.
- Next, feel the legs. Bring awareness to sensations arising from the skin and deep inside the legs. Notice any tingling, temperature, or numbness.
- Shift your attention up to feel the whole area of the pelvis, abdomen, and chest. Feel the breath, and feel any sensations of digestion, pressure, or heat.
- Feel the hands. Notice sensations in the palms, the fingers, and the backs of the hands. Attend to any numbness or movement in the hands.

(CONTINUED)

- Shift your attention to the arms and shoulders. Feel the surface of the skin, and feel deep into the muscles.
- Feel the neck, face, and head. Breathe with sensations arising from this region of the body. Notice any warmth, tightness, or ease.
- Finally, let your attention expand down from the head to include your whole body. Just feel the whole body, however it is in this moment. Allow this stillness and awareness to nourish you.

50. WHAT REALLY MATTERS?

🕐 10 minutes

In our impatience, it is easy to become hijacked by anxiety and restlessness. Instead of pausing and creating space to see clearly, we do the opposite, pushing even harder to be somewhere else. But where are we rushing, really? Caught up in this spiral, we lose touch with the bigger picture. Reflecting on our values can help us step back and see that the journey can be as rich as the destination.

- Find a comfortable seat where you feel awake and dignified. Allow your eyes to close, or gently gaze.
- Tune in to the sensations of the breath. Allow the breath to anchor you in this moment as you kindly let experiences come and go.
- Once settled, allow these questions to enter the mind:

  What matters most to me in life?

  What is my purpose for practicing mindfulness?

- Rather than thinking about the questions, see whether you can allow them to gently settle in the mind. You might allow them to drop like a stone tossed into a lake, slowly floating down through the cool, clear waters until it settles on the bottom.
- If thinking arises, see whether you can simply open up to whatever appears.

- As this practice comes to an end, take a moment to feel the body and the breath. If you did not arrive at any answers, that is okay. You may try this meditation again another time. If you did find answers, you may call upon what you noticed to gain new perspective.

---

51. BALANCING ACT

🕐 15 minutes 🖊 pen and paper

Sometimes our lives get out of balance, and in an effort to feel better, we either go into overdrive or shut down completely. Driven by stress, we often lose touch with the experiences that revitalize us. However, with patience, we can pause to look inward, considering what we truly need to care for ourselves. In this exercise from MBCT, we take a closer look at how we spend our time as we consider the balancing act of being human.

- Find a quiet place to reflect, and have a pen and paper with you.
- Start by making a list of what you do in your typical day. Give some detail. For example, rather than just write "work," indicate the major activities you do at work.
- Consider how each activity affects your mood and energy. Next to those activities that tend to fill you up, put an "N" for Nourishing. Next to those that tend to drain you, put a "D" for Depleting.
- Now count the number of Ns and Ds. There may be activities that can be N or D, depending on certain factors, and you can indicate that, too.
- Take a few moments to consider the following questions:

    Is there balance between Ns and Ds?

    Of the Ns, are there any you could do more frequently? Is there a way to bring more awareness to this nourishment?

    Of the Ds, are there any you could do less frequently? If not, is there a way to manage them so they have less impact on your mood?

(CONTINUED)

Of the activities that could be N or D, what factors determine their impact?

Are there any ways you might shift the activities of your day to take better care of yourself?

As you consider these questions, see whether you can drop your doing mind.

---

52. COUNTING TO TEN

🕑 5 minutes

Have you ever been told to "count to ten" when you're upset? Although counting is not a cure-all, taking a pause can interrupt our usual reactivity. It invites an opportunity to let things settle before we take action. Consider the question posed in the *Tao Te Ching*: "Do you have the patience to wait till your mud settles and the water is clear? Can you remain unmoving till the right action arises by itself?" When you become aware of strong emotions and an urge to act, try practicing this exercise before you do anything.

- Begin by sitting in a posture that makes you feel supported and awake. Gently close your eyes, or cast your gaze softly in front of you.
- Take a moment to notice how you are feeling and the urge you are experiencing. Maybe even label it. "I want to write an angry email," or "I want to eat those chips." Rate it on a scale of one to ten, with ten being an almost unbearably strong urge and one being easy to resist.
- Take a few deep breaths, and as you do this, notice where you feel the breath most clearly. As you let the breath return to normal, begin to rest your attention wherever it feels most prominent or pleasant. This might be at the nostrils, the chest, or the abdomen.
- As you pay attention to the sensations of breathing, count silently to yourself, "one" as you inhale and "one" as you exhale. Then count "two" as you inhale and "two" as you exhale. Continue to count in this way until you reach ten, and then start back at one.

- If you lose you count, simply start back at one, without judgment. Continue to count breaths. Notice when the mind gets pulled into thinking, and return to counting.
- As you complete this practice, notice how you feel and the strength of that urge. Rate it on a scale of one to ten.
- Congratulate yourself for allowing the water to clear before deciding how to proceed.

---

53. A CONSCIOUS PATH

🕒 3 minutes

We all have habitual ways of responding to difficult emotions. They are like a path we've worn through the woods over years of walking. But what if this path doesn't take us where we want to be? Carving out a new path takes intention and patience. It requires us to stop, investigate, and proceed with awareness. In this way, we can respond to difficulty fully informed by the present moment, rather than driven by habit.

- When you become aware of difficulty in the body or mind, see whether you can pause. Bring the body into an erect posture, signifying that you are coming into awareness of the present moment. You can keep your eyes open or gently close them. Take a few deep breaths to settle yourself.
- In step one of the breathing space, **turn your attention inward**. What is going on in the body? Without needing to change anything, gently take note of how the body feels. What emotions are present? Kindly acknowledge them and let them be. What is going on in the mind? Observe the thoughts passing through the mind.
- Once you have an idea of what is here, there is no need to do anything yet. Gently acknowledge how things are in this moment.

(CONTINUED)

- In step two of the breathing space, **focus on your breath**. Let things be as they are as you follow one breath and then the next.
- In step three of the breathing space, **expand your attention**. Feel the whole body in the fullness of the moment. Take a moment to be with your experience, aware of the sensations in your body and your breath. Allow the whole experience to be held in a softer and more expansive awareness.
- As this practice comes to an end, take a moment to consider how to proceed mindfully. Perhaps keep focusing on the breath, do some mindful movement, or write down any sticky thoughts. See whether you can allow your next actions to come from a place of responding rather than reacting.

54. MINDFUL CONVERSATION

🕐 5 minutes or as needed

As social beings, our need for connection, acceptance, and understanding is a powerful force. At the same time, we cannot control other people. Caught in this tension, we cultivate mindfulness and patience so we can approach our relationships—and challenging interactions—with more ease and grace. As Thich Nhat Hanh observed, "The most precious gift we can offer others is our presence. When our mindfulness embraces those we love, they will bloom like flowers."

- Choose an interaction that would benefit from greater awareness. Beforehand, find a moment to reflect on your intention to bring patience and awareness to the interaction.
- Take a few moments before the interaction to be aware. Start by feeling the body grounded on the surface you are sitting on. If you notice obvious tension, see if you can gently relax the body.
- Gather your attention and feel the sensations of the breath. Take a few deep breaths, and remember that the breath is always with you in each moment.

- As you begin the interaction, see whether you can maintain a gentle awareness of the breath and body in the background. This might look like giving three-quarters of your attention to speaking and listening and the remainder to feeling the breath and body.
- While listening, if you become aware of impatience arising, see whether you can very briefly slow down or pause. Focus more of your attention on the sensations of the breath, and take a few deeper breaths to settle the mind as you return to listening.
- While speaking, if you become aware of feeling tense, pressured, or irritated, see whether you can slow down or pause. Take a moment to quickly scan the body. Notice any bracing or holding, and gently relax to the degree that you can. Experiment with slowing down your rate of speech to see how this affects the interaction.
- If you become too upset to maintain awareness, see whether there is a way to peacefully exit the conversation.
- Take a few moments to notice the sensations of the body and breath as you expand your attention to the space around you and carry on with your day.

55. TAKING A NEW ROUTE

🕐 5 minutes

Imagine trying to take new route home from work after going the same way for years. It takes patience, intention, and probably a few hiccups to consistently follow the new route. Habitual patterns take patience and intention to redirect. Each time we get off track, if we pause and bring awareness to our experience, we can slowly change direction and move toward greater understanding and growth. Try this exercise when feeling pulled to react in old, habitual ways.

- Settle into a comfortable and alert seated posture, allowing your eyes to gently close. Take a moment to acknowledge whatever is pulling you toward a habitual reaction.

(CONTINUED)

- Shift to notice the sensations of the body sitting, and be aware of any tightness or contraction. Take note of any thoughts passing through the mind. There is no need to get caught up in the storyline. Perhaps simply label them, something like "self-critical thoughts" or "pleasant thoughts." See whether you can observe any emotions, and gently take note of them without any agenda to change them.
- For a few breaths, attend to the sensations as the air comes in and out. Take a natural breath in and, exhaling, say *patience*.
- See whether you can allow your experience to be as it is. For two to three minutes, practice inhaling normally and repeating *patience* as you exhale.
- If you find you have gotten pulled into thinking or distraction, gently let go and return to feeling the breath. Breathe in, and then breathe out *patience*, waiting for the urge to pass.
- As this practice comes to an end, kindly acknowledge any thoughts, emotions, or sensations that remain.
- As you proceed with your day, take a moment to feel the breath, and breathe out *patience* when you feel the familiar tug of old patterns.

56. SURROUNDED BY LOVE

◷ 10 minutes

Impatience is like being in a battle with your inner and outer circumstances. In this trance, we often perceive something insufficient about ourselves, our lives, or the present moment. Stuck in this fight, we lose sight of our wholeness and strength. Use this practice to reconnect with your own essential goodness.

- Sit comfortably, and let your eyes close or cast your gaze down softly. Take a minute to feel the body breathing, and allow thinking to fade into the background.

- When you are ready, bring to mind those in your life, now or in the past, who really appreciate and care for you. These could be teachers, animals, friends, children, mentors, or other loved ones. Allow them to be in your mind's eye.
- Take a few moments to reflect on the attention, kindness, and positive regard you have received from each of them. Imagine being encircled by these beings, receiving all their love and blessings for you. Feel their warmth.
- As you experience this sensation, silently repeat phrases that reflect this love and care from others. Allow these phrases to be your own, something like "may I be happy," "may I be free from harm," or "may I live with ease."
- See if it is possible to be open to receiving these wishes. Allow them to permeate and enter you fully.
- Kindly notice whatever arises as you continue to send this goodwill and care that you receive from others toward yourself.
- As this practice comes to an end, feel the whole length and breadth of the body. Recognize you are worthy of love, just as you are.

Words of Encouragement

Patience can feel fleeting. We have it one moment and the next it is gone. Every moment that we practice patience, we are clearing ground for a new path of acceptance and peace. When the brush seems especially thick, remind yourself that every painful experience you thought would last forever eventually ended.

Reflection

What did you notice as you worked through these meditations? What aspects of your experience stood out? How can you apply the attitude of patience to your daily life?

Mindfulness Meditations for Depression

When we sit so many thoughts and ideas and emotions come up. To gently note what's happening and then return to the breath is an acknowledgment that you trust the process of being.

—Noah Lampert, author, musician, and podcast host

CHAPTER SIX

Trust

The experience of depression can plant deep seeds of fear and self-doubt. In the midst of this experience, our usual ways of coping can fail us and add to our suffering. During these moments, it is easy to feel helpless and lose trust in ourselves. The more we spin out, the more we forget our own strength and goodness. We may even conclude that the problem is us (it is not!). Living in our heads, we become strangers to the present moment and to ourselves.

Yet relief can come when we turn to guidance from within. Trust comes from finding our way through the mental chatter so we can connect with our own inherent wisdom and resilience. In the present moment without judgment, we can develop the capacity to be with difficulty in our body and mind. As we learn to work with reactivity, bit by bit, we can develop a more intimate and trusting relationship with ourselves. Sadness, fear, and physical pain can wake us up and bring us closer to ourselves.

As we build trust in ourselves, we can increasingly depend on our intuition and inner resources for solace. This ability to rely on ourselves allows us to form more trusting relationships with others based on our own solid foundation.

Common Unhelpful Thoughts

There must be something wrong with me.

I am so weak.

I can't get things together.

57. BRAND-NEW DAY

(Mini-Meditation)

Upon first waking up in the morning, before you do anything, take a moment to reflect on your intention for the day. Rather than setting a goal, let it be a wish for *how* you would like to meet the day. *May I be aware and at ease. May I act with compassion for myself and others.* Whatever you choose, recite this intention silently, trusting yourself to meet whatever this new day offers you with awareness.

58. LEARNING FROM YOUR BREATH

🕐 5 minutes

When there is uncertainty, we often try to think and reason our way into feeling secure. In reality, this approach often fuels harmful rumination. With mindfulness, we can let go of the storyline and build trust from the inside out. As we cultivate the patience and compassion it takes to stay in the present moment, we can learn from our breath that each inhale and each exhale is an opportunity to come home to ourselves. We can start to trust ourselves, and we don't have to create a false sense of security through thinking.

- Begin this practice by finding a seated posture that allows you to feel dignified and awake to the present moment. Let your shoulders gently drop and your chest open as you close your eyes.
- Take a moment to feel the body supported by the earth. Kindly gather your attention and guide it here, into this moment, to feel the body sitting.
- As you attend to the body, you will become aware of the fact that you are breathing. Tune into your breath wherever it is clearest or most comfortable for you. See whether you can simply allow the breath to come and go, without intervening.
- Continue to follow the breath, and notice the brief pause at the end of the inhale before the body exhales, and the brief pause at the end of the exhale before the body inhales. See how the body does this all on its own.
- If you become aware that the mind has been pulled into thinking about your breath, the future, or the past, see whether you can gently let go of thinking and return to feel the next inhale and exhale.
- Know that you can always start fresh with a new inhale and a new exhale. See whether you can relax as you observe the breath coming in and out.
- As this practice comes to an end, take a moment to appreciate that our breath is always there to help unhook us from the thinking mind.

59. BEFRIENDING THE BODY

🕐 10 minutes

We tend to become aware of our body only when something is "wrong": We feel our heart racing in times of anxiety or our back aching after an injury, but we miss all that our body does "right." Without us having to do a thing, our lungs breathe, our heart beats, and our brain makes sense of the world. Greater awareness of our body, in all its states, can be healing. As author Mirka Knaster shares, "To connect with our bodies is to learn to trust ourselves, and from that comes power."

- Take a seat that feels comfortable, where you can be alert to the present moment. Allow your eyes to gently close, or gently cast your gaze onto the floor.
- Take a few deeper breaths before allowing the breath to return to its natural rhythm.
- Spend a few minutes following the sensations of the breath wherever you feel them most clearly. Carefully attend to the full length of the inhale and exhale.
- Know that your mind wandering is completely normal. When this happens, gently take note and guide your attention back to the breath.
- Now expand the awareness around the breath to feel a sense of the whole body sitting here. See whether you can fill the body with awareness and breath. Kindly observe the whole play of sensations as the body breathes.
- If any sensations arise that call for your attention, take a moment to investigate them. Bring your full attention to the sensations and notice their quality—their edges and any intensity or dissipation. Send the breath into and out of any discomfort you detect. See whether you can meet that intensity with interest and care.

- If specific sensations no longer call for your attention, gently let go and expand awareness back to the whole body. See whether you can hold your body in a warm and patient awareness, appreciating it in all its complexity.
- As this practice ends, take a moment to anchor your attention on the breath again before expanding your awareness to the space around you.

---

60. LEAVES FLOATING BY

🕐 10 minutes

Self-doubt undermines trust in ourselves. When we watch closely, we see that more thinking is rarely the answer to our insecurities—ruminating on self-doubt generally fuels it. Instead, we need to dig deep. When we work to build trust from the inside out, we can access a deep sense of steadiness that builds self-trust below the level of thinking. It takes a leap of faith to drop the storyline and access the wisdom below. Here is a way to start.

- Take a seat that feels steady and comfortable. Allow your eyes to close, or let your gaze rest softly in front of you.
- Begin by feeling your seated posture. Notice where the body is held by the surface on which you sit. Let yourself arrive in this moment.
- Spend a few minutes feeling the sensations of the breath. Allow your attention to rest wherever you feel the breath most clearly. For now, just notice when thinking arises, gently label it "thinking," and then come back to the breath.
- Now shift your attention to purposefully become aware of thoughts. Imagine you are sitting on the edge of a stream. See whether you can notice each thought that arises, place it on a leaf, and allow it to float by.
- If you find yourself swept up in the storyline, see whether you can let go and return to noticing thoughts. Return to the edge of the stream. Regardless of what the thoughts are—enthusiastic or judging—place

(CONTINUED)

each one on a leaf and allow it to continue on its way downstream. If there is an emotional charge or physical sensation accompanying the thought, gently take note before letting it go.

- Finally, take a minute to let go of thinking and focus on the breath. Follow the sensations as the breath comes in and out.
- As this practice ends, acknowledge your efforts. Know that even if you missed a thought or got pulled into the thought stream, this practice of noticing is strengthening your ability to trust your awareness.

61. OPEN TO THE FLOW

🕐 10 minutes

Without the distance that awareness brings, we are pulled like a magnet to whatever thoughts, emotions, or urges arise. When this happens, we lose the ability to see clearly and to choose responses that align with our deepest values. Trust in ourselves erodes. The more we can open to the natural flow of our experience—including patterns of self-doubt, separateness, and unworthiness—the more we regain the space to take it all a bit less personally and act with intention.

- Find a posture that is comfortable and upright. Allow your eyes to gently close, or cast your gaze softly in front of you.
- Take a moment to tune into the sensations of sitting here. Feel the body resting on the chair or the cushion. Arrive here.
- For a few minutes, shift your attention to sensations of the breath. Carefully follow the sensations as the body breathes in and out.
- When you are ready, allow the breath to fade into the background, expanding awareness to include the whole moment. Open to all experiences as they enter and leave your awareness.
- If sounds arise, kindly note them. If thoughts arise, label them "thinking." Each time, gently let go and return to the present moment.

- If you get caught up in one aspect of your experience, gently let go and relax back into awareness. Relax with the natural flow of experience.
- Notice each experience that arises without judgment. There is no need to hold on or push away.
- For the last few moments of this practice, allow your attention to return to the breath. Whatever you became aware of during this practice, congratulate yourself for your efforts to open to the flow.

62. MOMENT-TO-MOMENT MOVEMENT

🕐 10 minutes

One important place to cultivate trust is within our own bodies. When we are connected, we develop wisdom about our bodies that can help us care for ourselves. You know your experience better than anyone else, after all. However, distracted by depressive thoughts or driven by aversion, we often look outside ourselves for insight that can only be found by looking inward. In this practice, we observe our moment-to-moment experience of movement. In touch with our body, we can learn to trust our inner strength and honor our limits.

- Begin this practice in a place where you have room to spread out. Make sure you are wearing comfortable clothing. You may choose to have a yoga mat for extra support. Although there are instructions for each movement, try to look inward for what is available to your individual body. The intention is to breathe and move with continuous awareness, however it is that you comfortably move.
- If it's possible and comfortable, start by lying on your back on a mat or soft surface. Allow your arms and legs to be long and your eyes to gently close. Feel the whole body lying here.

(CONTINUED)

- Allow your feet to rest on the mat with your knees pointing toward the sky. Your arms can be alongside you or in a T. On your next inhale, arch your lower back slightly so it moves away from the floor, pelvis tilting down. On your exhale, bring your lower back to meet the floor, pelvis tilting up. Continue these gentle movements for a few breaths, just noticing what this feels like.
- Now slowly bring your knees up toward your chest, grabbing hold of your knees if possible. Feel the sensations this creates, and allow any movements that feel right to you.
- Release your left leg so it is long on the mat, or place your left foot flat on the ground with your knee bent. With your left leg either straight or bent, gently squeeze your right knee into your chest.
- With awareness, switch legs so you are gently hugging your left knee.
- Now place both feet flat on the floor with your knees bent and your arms in a T. Slowly allow both knees to fall toward the right and, if possible and comfortable, gently look toward the left.
- Bring your knees back to center and then allow them to fall to the left while you gently look toward the right.
- Allow your knees to come to the center once again, and then let your legs be long with your arms alongside your body, palms facing up.
- As this practice ends, take a moment to rest here in stillness, feeling the sensations of the body. Be careful to support your body with your arms as you move to a seated position.

63. OUR PLACE IN NATURE

🕐 10 minutes

In the throes of strong emotions and sticky thoughts, we can easily start to feel separate and deficient. Swept away in our suffering, we lose sight of our common humanity with others and our connection with the earth. We forget that we are part of something much greater and wiser than our limited thinking minds. Something as simple as going outside can shift our perspective and open us up to belonging to a wider world.

- Find a time when you can be out in nature for a few minutes. Choose somewhere you can walk and take in something natural, like a tree, a stream, plants, or grass.
- Begin this practice by taking a few deeper breaths to help you arrive in this moment. Then begin to slowly walk. As you walk, tune in to your senses and take in your surroundings. See whether you can relax and simply observe colors, textures, light, and shapes. Perhaps notice scents or sounds arising as you take in the environment.
- If you find you have gotten pulled into thinking, labeling, or judging, let go and see whether you can return to directly sensing nature.
- Carefully tune in to experience the moment with curiosity, paying great attention to detail. Bring a sense of beginner's mind as you take in the natural world.
- As you continue to walk, consider the trust you have in nature to unfold all on its own. Without us doing a thing, the seasons arrive, flowers bloom, water flows, and tides change.
- As you complete this practice, take a moment to feel the air on your skin and know that you have a place in nature.

64. WISE MIND

🕐 10 minutes

We all possess a sense of wisdom and intuition. Even if we have not accessed it for a time, it is there, like water at the bottom of a deep abandoned well. As we find the balance between our doing mind and our being mind, we can begin to reconnect with our own wise mind. The following practice is intended to help that process. You can try practicing it when you are struggling to trust

(CONTINUED)

yourself. Start with something mildly challenging before using it in more intense situations.

- Begin by finding a quiet place to sit. Allow the body to be supported and upright, with a sense of dignity. You can close your eyes or gently cast your gaze downward.
- Start by feeling your body sitting here. Notice where the body is grounded and supported by the surface you are sitting on, and feel it rise upward, like a deeply rooted tree or a mountain.
- Now begin to notice the fact that you are breathing.
- As you breathe in completely, feel the sensations of your breath coming in. As you breathe out, allow your attention to settle down from your head into your center, perhaps at your solar plexus. Let your attention move down from your head to fill the body. Continue breathing in this way until you feel your attention settle and drop into your center.
- Keep your attention in this region as you breathe normally. Breathing in, ask the wise mind a question, like *What should I do?* Breathing out, listen for the answer. Continue this for a time. Rather than telling yourself the answer, wait for the answer to arise. If nothing becomes clear, ask again later.
- As this practice ends, take a few moments to rest in this balanced and centered awareness.

65. LISTENING TO THE BODY

When reflecting with a recent MBCT group on why it is helpful to step out of autopilot throughout the day, one patient shared that she typically gets home in the evening and feels unable to function. Once she started to pay more attention, she realized that she was so in her head throughout the day that she would forget to do things like eat and drink water. When we ignore our needs, we suffer mentally and physically. By paying more attention, we can build trust in our body, as we learn to give it what it needs to support us.

- Choose a day when you intend to check in on your body. If you can, set an alarm for every two to three hours to support this awareness.
- When your reminder goes off, take a moment to briefly scan the body. Feel any stiffness, soreness, or hunger. Take a moment to be with the sensations, considering what a caring response might be to what you notice. Continue on with what you are doing, or perhaps pause and choose to engage in self-care. You might stand up and stretch or get a drink of water. Allow your actions to be responsive and compassionate.
- See whether you notice any resistance to this slowing down, and gently note any thoughts, judgments, or emotions that arise. Allow whatever arises to be there as you get in touch with your intention to develop greater trust and intimacy with your body.
- Each time you are reminded, see whether you can bring a sense of curiosity and care to tuning in to the body. Notice any tightness, ease, or clenching. Take a moment to observe whatever you become aware of and notice whether any appropriate action reveals itself. Maybe switch to a new task, take a short mindful walk, or get a snack.
- At the end of the day, reflect on what you noticed as you checked in with your body. See how you feel. If this practice was helpful, see whether you can carry it forward.

66. DROP BELOW THINKING

🕐 10 minutes

Have you ever been stuck trying to solve a problem only to have the answer come to you when you finally let it go and do something else? You go for a walk, take a bath, or pet your dog, and—BAM!—there it is. This same process can happen when it comes to difficult emotions. Without a sense of trust in ourselves, we can easily get caught up in a merry-go-round of thinking. In this

(CONTINUED)

practice, we build trust as we find the courage to drop below thinking, even letting go mid-thought, and allow a deeper knowing to arise.

- Adopt a posture that feels comfortable while enabling you to remain alert and awake. Allow your eyes to close, or cast your gaze softly downward.
- Take a minute to feel the sensations of sitting. Notice any sense of pressure or touch where your body meets the surface you are sitting on. Feel where your hands rest on your legs or lap.
- Spend a minute or two observing the breath. Allow the breath to bring you into this moment.
- Know that thoughts are not the enemy, so for now, if they arise, gently take note of them and guide your attention back to your breath.
- Now purposefully allow a minor problem or irritation into the mind. Take a moment to simply allow the mind to do what it wants, and notice whatever thinking arises.
- Inhale. Then, on the exhale, purposefully let go of thinking and anchor your attention on the body.
- Continue to sit with a sense of the body. Whenever thinking arises, practice letting go of thinking on the inhale and being with the body on the exhale. See whether you can breathe as you kindly acknowledge any sensations that arise, knowing what it feels like to drop below thinking info feeling.
- As this practice ends, regardless of whether some clarity or solution arose, take a moment to congratulate yourself for your efforts to trust.

67. TRUSTING IMPERMANENCE

⏱ 3 minutes

When we are in the thick of discomfort or uncertainty, it can seem that things will never get better. In meditation, as we watch the ever-changing play of our experience, we learn trust in the power of time to heal; we become more aware of our ability to hold pain. Whenever I feel like difficult feelings will last forever, I like to remind myself of this Pali chant I heard at my first silent meditation retreat:

> *All things are impermanent*
> *They arise, and they pass away*
> *To live in harmony with this truth*
> *Brings great happiness.*

We can use mindfulness to help us remember the impermanent nature of our experiences. When you become aware of difficulty in body or mind, see whether you can take three minutes to pause and use this exercise to meet the difficulty with awareness.

- Signal stepping into the present moment by bringing your body into an upright and dignified posture. You can let your eyes close or allow your gaze to be soft and cast downward.
- First, take one minute to **turn your attention inward** to notice your experience right now. Let go of needing to do anything about it as you take note of any sensations, emotions, or thoughts that are present. Once you have a sense of your experience, perhaps say, *Okay, this is how it is right now.*
- For one minute, **focus on your breath** to ground yourself in this moment. Gently let thoughts, feelings, and emotions fade into the background as you bring the breath center stage in your awareness. Focus on feeling the changing pattern of sensations of the breath.
- For one minute, **expand your attention** around your breath to feel the whole body sitting here breathing. In this spacious awareness, notice any remaining tension or difficulty as it rises and passes away. Perhaps take a moment to send breath into and out of any contraction or holding in your body. On the exhale, gently say to yourself, *softening, opening.* Allow the experience to unfold naturally.
- As you complete this practice, see whether you can bring this more allowing awareness into the next moments of your day.

68. GREETING UNCERTAINTY WITH COMPASSION

🕐 10 minutes

When we are faced with the unknown, our need for control often takes over, leading us to predictions about the future or rumination about past losses. Yet when we accept that uncertainty and difficulty are unavoidable parts of life, we can learn to override our fear and instead greet what comes with a steadier stance. Tara Brach provides a helpful framework for awakening this awareness with compassion in a process called RAIN:

- Find a comfortable and alert seated posture. Allow your eyes to gently close, or cast your gaze softly downward.
- Feel the body grounded on your seat, noticing any points of contact or pressure.
- Spend a few minutes following the sensations of the breath. Allow the breath to be just as it is.
- Bring to mind an uncertainty you struggle with. This could be a current difficulty like waiting to hear about a job, or a long-standing struggle like the future of a relationship. Allow it to be in your mind for a moment.
- Now turn your attention inward and:
    - **Recognize** what is going on. Take a few moments to acknowledge your experience in this moment. See if you can gently label thoughts, feelings, and urges arising for you.
    - **Allow** the experience to be there, just as it is. See whether you can take a moment to notice any urges to fix or change your experience and simply let it be. You might even say to yourself, *It's okay to feel this*, *This belongs*, or *Yes*.
    - **Investigate** with interest and care. See whether you can cultivate a sense of curiosity about your experience. Perhaps ask, *What most wants attention?* or *How am I experiencing this in my body?* Gently step away from thinking and move into a felt sense of the body.

- **Nurture** with self-compassion. As you recognize the reality of this suffering, see whether you can offer yourself kindness and self-care. Perhaps place a gentle touch on any difficulty felt in your body, or offer yourself a phrase of caring, like *Trust in your goodness*. If it feels challenging to offer this caring to yourself, perhaps envision someone you care about offering this compassion and love to you.
- As you complete the RAIN practice, take a moment to sense your experience in this moment. Acknowledge that by being with your experience in this way, you are letting go of a limited sense of self and cultivating trust. Know that you can use these steps with other difficulties in meditation or as they arise in life.

69. SENDING AND RECEIVING

🕐 10 minutes

We build trust in ourselves as we see our ability to meet life as it is. More aware and less attached, we start to let go of our habitual tendencies to seek pleasure and avoid pain. The Tibetan practice of sending and receiving called *tonglen* challenges these tendencies by inhaling pain and suffering and exhaling love, ease, or whatever quality is needed. When we can meet pain in this way, we become a spiritual warrior, using our own personal suffering to cultivate compassion for all who suffer.

- Find a steady and open seated posture. Allow your eyes to gently close, or cast your gaze softly downward.
- Take a few deep breaths, and allow the body and mind to settle. Spend a minute or two feeling the body sit in stillness.
- Bring to mind a place of pain or struggle in your life. Perhaps you have been experiencing feelings of inadequacy, lack of motivation, or hopelessness.

(CONTINUED)

- Breathe in, focusing on the weight and darkness of this pain. Imagine yourself breathing in this suffering. Perhaps envision breathing in heat, darkness, and heaviness.
- Breathe out, focusing on soothing, happiness, and ease. Perhaps envision breathing out coolness, light, and weightlessness.
- As you continue this practice, breathe in any pain, negativity, or suffering and exhale whatever healing or kindness is needed. Know that the suffering is not staying, but rather moving through you and coming out as ease and love.
- As you do this, you might expand this practice to include all those who are in the same boat as you, living with the same pain, feelings of inadequacy, or hopelessness. Breathe in their suffering and send out healing, relief, and support to those in need.
- As this practice comes to an end, take a few moments to let go of any particular focus of attention and simply sit with a sense of your whole body, holding it in kind and receptive awareness.
- If this practice was helpful, allow it to be a tool to face suffering with compassion.

70. LOVING OUR IMPERFECTIONS

🕐 10 minutes

Imagine if someone was constantly doubting, judging, and criticizing you. How much would you be able to trust them? Now think about yourself and how a critical inner dialogue erodes trust in ourselves. As Pema Chödrön describes it, "The most fundamental aggression to ourselves, the most fundamental harm we can do to ourselves, is to remain ignorant by not having the courage and the respect to look at ourselves honestly and gently." We are all imperfect. In this exercise, we directly acknowledge our imperfections with compassion.

- Begin this practice by finding a comfortable and quiet place to sit. Allow your body to be upright and relaxed. You can let your eyes gently close or cast your gaze softly on the floor.
- To start, feel the body sitting here in this moment. Gently notice any sensations of touch, pressure, or contact. Gather your attention and arrive here.
- Next, bring to mind a perceived inadequacy or imperfection you often struggle with. Notice the story of imperfection you are telling yourself.
- Become aware of any emotions that arise and gently label them. Notice any sensations that arise in the body as you become aware of this story of inadequacy.
- Take a moment to reflect on this story as if a close friend or loved one was in the same situation. What would you say to them?
- As you do this, take a few minutes to repeat the following phrases quietly to yourself. Feel free to modify the phrases so they resonate with you:

    May I be kind to myself

    May I accept myself just as I am

    May I meet my imperfections with loving-kindness

- Any time your attention gets pulled into thinking or other distractions, gently let go and return to these phrases.
- Kindly and patiently notice any sensations that arise as you do this practice. Know that even it feels clunky at first, this intention to greet our imperfections with acceptance is building trust within ourselves.

71. SHINE ON

© 10 minutes

As our habitual patterns become clearer, we can begin to take them less personally. When we identify less with the stories we repeat about ourselves and instead tune into the reality of our experience, we can appreciate our goodness and uniqueness. This is how self-trust emerges. Eckhart Tolle tells us, "The source of all abundance is not outside you. It is part of who you are."

- Find a quiet place and a comfortable seat. Allow your body to be upright and relaxed. Let your eyes close, or gently cast your gaze downward.
- Take a minute to connect with the sensations of the breath. Rest your attention on the length of the inhale and the length of the exhale. Relax into the moment.
- When you feel settled, bring to mind someone who loves and trusts you, regardless of whether you think their trust is warranted. Imagine this person and their trust in you. Feel their trust radiating from them to you. Breathe with any sensation this creates. Allow yourself to sense and take in their love and positive regard for you.
- Now bring to mind a time when you felt some sense of certainty or trust in yourself. Perhaps reflect on a time when you made a decision or took action from a place of trust and wisdom. See whether you can feel it within your body and invite it to grow.
- Take a moment to consider how when it is raining and cloudy, it appears at first glance that there is no sunshine. However, if you fly high above the clouds, you will see that the sun *is* still shining. Your inability to see it does not mean it is not there. In much the same way, even when we feel unsteady or insecure, our true nature is still there behind the clouds, waiting to shine through again.

Words of Encouragement

When we are distant from ourselves, it is hard to build trust in our capacity to skillfully meet what life offers us. Why would we confide in a stranger? As you practice mindfulness, each experience you have—pleasant and unpleasant—becomes an opportunity to trust in your ability to be aware, to be here. As you get to know your moment-to-moment experience, and even befriend it, you are nourishing the soil for self-trust to grow.

Reflection

What did you notice as you worked through these meditations? What aspects of your experience stood out? How can you apply the attitude of trust to your daily life?

Mindfulness Meditations for Depression

Mindfulness Meditations for Depression

We do so much, we run so quickly, the situation is difficult, and many people say, "Don't just sit there, do something." But doing more things may make the situation worse. So you should say, "Don't just do something, sit there." Sit there, stop, be yourself first, and begin from there.

—Thich Nhat Hanh, Buddhist teacher, poet, and activist

CHAPTER SEVEN

Non-striving

Striving adds suffering to depression as we compare where we are to where we think we should be. As Thich Nhat Hanh describes in the opening chapter quote, sometimes doing more things actually worsens depression. When depression shows up, it is easy to want to fix things with fighting, ignoring, judging, and "shoulds." Once these habits take hold, what starts as a low mood can quickly spiral into something much worse. These are the toughest yet most critical moments in which to turn our attention toward whatever the present moment holds.

Non-striving does not mean that we do not have goals or hopes. It is natural to want to be happy and well. Rather, non-striving means we notice how our attachments cause us suffering. We acknowledge that running around trying to control everything does not help us achieve a true sense of peace. In the case of depression, non-striving means acknowledging sadness, fatigue, or disinterest with kindness and without judgment.

Through this acknowledgment, we make space for these negative experiences to unfold without the added distress caused by our resistance. It frees up energy to see the moment more clearly, including the inevitability of change. This is quite the opposite of being stagnant or passive. It is the active decision to be with the moment as it is so we can choose actions that will be most helpful and responsive.

Common Unhelpful Thoughts

Why can't I ever succeed?

I am so disappointed in myself.

Everyone else has gotten it together. Why can't I?

---

72. GROUNDED

🕐 5 minutes

Striving can leave us living in the future, feeling scattered and even detached from our present selves and our lives. When we learn to ground ourselves, we loosen this habit and foster the ability to connect to the present moment, wherever we are.

- You can try this practice standing up, or feel free to do it sitting down if that feels best. Allow your feet to be hips-width apart, and let your arms hang loosely by your sides. If it is okay for you, allow your eyes to gently close.
- Begin by taking a few deeper breaths as you allow the body to settle and relax to the degree that it will.
- Let the breath return to normal, and start to slowly move your attention down the body until it settles into your feet.
- Take a few moments to simply be with the sensations in the feet. Feel the weight of the body and the pressure where your feet meet the ground.

- Begin to imagine yourself as a strong and steady tree. Feel your body as the trunk of the tree rising gracefully upward, and feel your feet as the base of the tree meeting the earth.
- As you stand here, imagine you are growing roots from the soles of your feet. Let the roots slowly reach down into the earth.
- If thoughts or emotions arise, let them simply come and go like wind passing though the branches of the tree. Perhaps the branches sway, but the tree remains firmly rooted in the earth.
- Continue to breathe as you imagine your roots growing deeper and deeper toward the center of the earth, solid, secure, and balanced.
- For the last few minutes of this practice, simply rest with the feeling of being fully grounded and present in this moment.

73. BEING BREATHING

🕐 10 minutes

One of the most challenging aspects of mindfulness is understanding that although it requires effort, it is not about achieving a particular outcome or state. It is about learning to let go of needing things to be other than they are so that we can be with each moment with greater ease. The great tension that arises is that we secretly want meditation to "work" for us. We are attached to the outcome, practicing for greater peace, clarity, or connection. Non-striving can help ensure meditation doesn't become one more reason to be hard on ourselves.

- Find a comfortable seated posture that feels dignified and alert. Let your eyes gently close, or cast your gaze softly on the floor.
- As you settle in, tune in to the sensations of sitting here. Feel the points where the body meets the chair or cushion. See whether you can take a moment and allow sitting here to be good enough. Nothing else needs to happen.

(CONTINUED)

- Shift your attention to the sensations of breathing. Notice how breathing is already happening, and you don't need to do anything.
- If the doing mind arises—wanting to achieve a certain state or get better at meditation—simply notice this happening. Gently relax back into feeling the body breathe.
- Can you allow yourself to just be present with each inhale and each exhale?
- As you breathe, you might notice sounds, thoughts, and sensations. If you can, allow them to simply go on in the background while you attend to the breath. You do not need to do anything about them. Whatever is, is enough.
- As this practice comes to an end, take a moment to honor yourself for sitting.

74. LET IT FLOW

🕐 15 minutes

When we are overly attached to things being a certain way, we end up on a roller coaster. When things go our way, we feel good. When they don't, we are down. This applies to our inner experience, too. Feeling down is challenging enough, but when you add the attitude of wanting it to change, it becomes unworkable. Much of our experience is outside of our control. In this exercise, we practice non-striving as we open to different aspects of our experience and let it flow.

- Find a seated posture that feels comfortable and awake to the present moment. You can let your eyes gently close or cast your gaze softly downward.
- Take a few deep breaths and pay attention to where you feel the breath most clearly. Allow the breath to return to normal, and begin to follow the sensations of the breath wherever it feels clearest to you. Take a few minutes to let it flow in and out naturally.
- When you notice your attention is no longer on the breath, take note of where the mind has gone, gently returning your attention to the

breath. Remember that it is quite normal for the mind to wander; there is no need to get rid of thoughts.

- Let go of breathing, and shift your attention to noticing sounds. Notice how sounds are happening all on their own. There is nothing to do but simply open up to receiving sounds. Take a few minutes to simply allow them to come and go in your awareness.
- Now, let go of sounds, and shift your attention to noticing thoughts. In the same way you observed sounds, begin to see thoughts as they arise and pass away.
- If it is helpful, perhaps imagine thoughts as clouds passing through the open sky of the mind. Notice how some clouds are quite light and pass by quickly, and others may be heavier and pass by more slowly.
- If you find that thoughts bring with them an emotional charge, you can notice that, too, and perhaps see whether you detect the emotion anywhere in the body. Then gently let go and relax once again to observe thoughts.
- As this practice comes to an end, let go of thoughts and spend a moment feeling the breath once again. Breathe in, knowing that you are breathing in. Breathe out, knowing that you are breathing out.

75. GOODBYE AGENDAS

🕐 10 minutes

Without awareness, we can get so caught up in the stories we repeat about ourselves—how we are or should be—that we lose touch with our true selves. Conversely, we build steadiness and confidence by being in touch with the actuality of our experience, no matter how messy it is. When we know ourselves better, including our habitual reactions, we are practicing non-striving. With this body scan, we can begin to let go of any agenda and take time to be ourselves.

- Begin by finding a quiet place to practice where you won't be interrupted.

(CONTINUED)

- Find a comfortable posture either lying down or seated in a chair. You can allow your eyes to gently close or let your gaze be soft.
- Begin by attending to the sensations of the whole body sitting or lying here. Take a minute to simply be just as you are and feel the sensations where the body is supported by the surface you are on.
- Next, connect with the sensations of the breath at the belly. Feel the breath as it comes in and out, letting it be natural. Remember as you move through this practice that there is no right or wrong way to pay attention.
- If you notice thoughts about what you should be doing with this time or how you should be feeling, see whether you can gently label these thoughts "striving" and return your attention to the body.
- Now guide your attention as if it were a spotlight down to the feet. Spend a few moments investigating the changing pattern of sensations in the feet. There's nothing to do but kindly take note of sensations.
- Shift your attention to feel the lower legs. Notice sensations arising from the skin and deep inside the legs as you breathe. If there are no sensations, that's okay. Just rest your attention on the lower legs.
- Shift your attention to the upper legs and pelvis. Feel deep into the muscles and bones. Notice sensations as they arise, shift, change, or stay the same.
- Shift your attention to the abdomen, chest, back, and shoulders. Feel the whole center of the body, perhaps noticing the movement of the breath or where the body meets the chair or the mat.
- Shift your attention to the arms and hands. Attend to any sensations arising from this region of the body. Notice any movement or temperature.
- Shift your attention up to feel the face. Notice any sensations of tension or holding.
- Finally, expand your attention to include the whole body sitting or lying here in this moment. Perhaps you can feel a sense that your whole body is breathing. Let go of any agenda as you hold the body in a kind and friendly awareness.

- As this practice comes to an end, bring some gentle movement into the body, and if you are lying down, be sure to support yourself as you come to a sitting position.

76. KISS THE JOY

🕐 10 to 15 minutes

Attachment to pleasant experiences can pull us into a cycle of constant desire, seeking the next moment of relief or pleasure. In this vicious cycle, we are so caught up in striving that we miss the very thing we have been looking for. I still sometimes find myself out in nature, struck by some beauty, having the urge to take a picture to "capture" it. Paradoxically, this need to hold on to the moment takes us out of it. As the poet William Blake reminds us:

> *He who binds to himself a joy*
> *Does the winged life destroy*
> *But he who kisses the joy as it flies*
> *Lives in eternity's sun rise.*

- Choose an activity you consider pleasurable, enjoyable, or nourishing. This activity could be anything, but some examples are eating a food you like, spending time in nature, listening to music, or taking a bath. You might want to choose something lasting a discrete amount of time, ten to fifteen minutes.
- Before you begin, take a moment to connect with your intention to be fully aware and awake to the present moment. Know that if thoughts arise, you can gently note them and return to attending fully to your senses.
- See whether you can throw yourself into the moment completely. Take in the sights, smells, sounds, tastes, and sensations.

(CONTINUED)

- If you notice thoughts about how great this is, thoughts about how you want to feel this way more often, or other thoughts about a desire to "capture" the moment, see whether you can gently let go and return to truly experience the moment in all its fullness.
- As this practice comes to an end, see whether you can connect with a sense of appreciation for your experience and let it go.

77. LISTENING TO LIMITS

🕐 10 minutes

There are so many ways our bodies can teach us about non-striving. As much as we may try to control it or resist it, time goes on and the body ages. Fighting this truth is most certainly a losing battle. Not only does our appearance change with age, but our physical limitations also change depending on the day. Learning to listen kindly to the changing limits of our body is good practice for cultivating non-striving. With this attitude, we can connect with a deeper appreciation and respect for our body and the storms it has weathered.

- Begin in a standing posture with your feet hips-width apart. If possible, try these movements without shoes. Before you begin, remember that the intention of this practice is not to get fit or achieve any particular outcomes. Rather, see whether you can bring a deep awareness to the body and the sensations created as you move, however it is that you comfortably move. Be sure to carefully attend to your limits, and adapt the movements to fit your needs.
- Spend a moment feeling the body standing here at rest and in stillness. Notice the whole length and breadth of the body as you breathe.
- When you are ready, on an inhale, lift your heels so that you are on the balls of your feet, and on the exhale, lower your heels back down slowly, allowing your toes to lift slightly. Repeat this movement for ten breaths, using a chair or wall for balance if needed.
- Come to stillness. Just rest in awareness of the changing pattern of sensations as you breathe.

- Next, on an inhale, bring your arms to a T position. As you exhale, reach your right arm up overhead and let your left arm come down as you lean to your left. As you inhale, bring your arms back to a T, and as you exhale again, lift your left arm up overhead and let your right arm come down as you lean to the right. Repeat this movement for ten breaths, pausing for a break or coming back to stillness as needed.
- Take a moment to feel the aftereffects of this movement. Rest in awareness of the body.
- Making sure you have some room around you, start to slowly swing your arms like a helicopter from side to side. Keep your feet planted, and allow your body to gently twist. Continue this for about ten breaths.
- Finally, allow the body to come to stillness once more, and simply feel your body standing here. Take a moment to cultivate some gratitude for the body just as you find it.

---

78. ARRIVE IN EACH MOMENT

🕐 10 minutes

Our constant desire to get somewhere can be addictive and exhausting. On the one hand, we feel productive and perhaps accomplished. On the other, we are distracted from the present moment, constantly moving but never truly arriving. We are doing the work without enjoying the fruits of our labor. In this mindful walking exercise, we see what it is like instead to arrive in each moment. As the Buddhist scholar Wu-Men writes:

> *Ten thousand flowers in spring, the moon in autumn,*
> *a cool breeze in summer, snow in winter.*
> *If your mind isn't clouded by unnecessary things,*
> *this is the best season of your life.*

(CONTINUED)

- Find a place outside where you can walk for five to ten minutes. It can help to find a place that is uncrowded. Feel free to adapt this practice to your own mobility needs, with comfortable, mindful movement as your only "goal."
- Before you begin, take a moment to stand in an upright and relaxed posture and feel the body standing here. Kindly note the sensations of the body and the breath.
- Acknowledge the intention to be present for each movement and each step. See whether you can let go of needing to get anywhere or be a certain way. Open up with curiosity to the actual experience of this moment.
- Begin to transfer your weight onto your right leg, noticing the changing pattern of sensations in the foot as you do so. Then slowly lift the left foot and gently move it forward and place it down.
- Shift your weight onto your left leg, attending to the sensation this shift creates. Then, with awareness, lift the right foot and slowly move it forward and place it down.
- Continue to walk slowly in the way. If you notice your attention is no longer on walking, pause and gently gather your attention by seeing what is around you, taking a breath, and returning once again at the sensations of walking.
- See whether you can let go of where you are going and how far you will walk, so you zoom to your direct experience of walking. See whether you can arrive in each moment.
- Continue on in this way until this practice feels complete. Let go of the "right" way to do it or any sense of pushing or trying too hard, and simply finish when you feel ready.

79. TURN INTO THE SKID

🕐 10 minutes

The idea of choosing to turn toward and gently investigate what is difficult seems to go against our instincts. However, in turning away too quickly, we never get a clear sense of the difficulty itself, and we may struggle to respond wisely. Turning toward difficulty reminds me of driving in winter. When the back of the car slides out one way, it is only by turning the wheel toward rather than away from the skid that the driver maintains control of the car. In the following exercise, we investigate this counterintuitive turning toward.

- Find a seated posture that feels steady and alert. You can let your eyes gently close or leave your eyes open with your gaze soft.
- Notice the sensations of sitting here in this moment. Feel the weight of the body on the surface you are sitting on.
- Now begin to notice thoughts. Is there some problem you are trying to solve? Some uncertainty or discomfort you are trying to fix or figure out?
- Take a moment to allow the problem into the mind. Without thinking about it, simply acknowledge it and allow it to be there.
- See whether you notice a pull to find a solution or fix the problem and gently label this pull "striving."
- Now, see if you can turn toward the problem itself to see it more clearly.
- Notice any discomfort that arises, in body or mind. What thoughts and emotions come along with this situation? See whether you can meet whatever arises with patience and understanding, maybe saying, *Ah, thoughts about the future*, or *Yes, the feeling of anxiety.*
- As you rest in awareness of this problem, turn your attention to the body to detect any sensations arising. See how this problem is felt in the body. Let go of any story in the mind as you attend to the sensations, kindly exploring them as you breathe.

(CONTINUED)

- Continue to breathe into any sensations you find, and as you breathe out, silently repeat to yourself *softening, opening.* Continue to do this as a gesture of welcoming.
- As this practice comes to an end, let go of any particular focus of attention within the body, and feel the whole body sitting here.
- Take a moment to acknowledge your courage to turn into the skid and know your experience more fully.

80. LEAVING WORRY BEHIND

One of the great challenges we face as humans is confronting the illusion of control. Uncertainty often drags us into rumination as we try to gain some sense of control. Yet doing the very opposite—acknowledging the limits of our control, and learning to unhook from thinking—saves our limited energy and keeps us from spiraling downward. This reminds me of the final stanza from "I Worried," a poem by Mary Oliver:

> *Finally I saw that worrying had come to nothing.*
> *And gave it up. And took my old body*
> *and went out into the morning,*
> *and sang.*

- Choose a day when you intend to be aware of worrying as it arises.
- See whether you can notice when you begin to worry. You might notice your mind racing or your body tensing. You also might notice feeling distracted or withdrawn.
- When this happens, see whether you can turn inward and identify what you are worrying about. In other words, without judgment, name the topic of your worry: maybe "worrying about being liked" or "worrying about the weather."
- Next, take a moment to feel the breath and the body and notice how this worry is affecting you physically. Spend a minute simply breathing with the sensations in the body.

- Then, ask yourself, *Is this a worry I can control or realistically benefit from acting on? Or is this outside of the limits of what I can reasonably control?*
- Take a moment to consider your answer and determine how you would like to proceed. Acknowledge how things are in this moment. Choose a way of responding that feels wise to you.

81. GETTING UNSTUCK

🕐 5 minutes

Our tendency to strive for comfort often gets us stuck; we find that we cannot skip over the hard parts if we want to live a life that we value. Life requires us to be with uncertainty and difficult emotions. By pausing to notice our striving, we can break the cycle of avoidance that brings us further from what we truly desire. Try this exercise when you are feeling stuck and wanting things to be different than they are.

- Start off this practice by bringing the body into a posture that signals being present and aware. You can perform this practice with your eyes open or closed.
- Take a few deeper breaths to settle your attention. Notice any urgency to do something and see whether you can let go. Commit to bringing a warm and patient awareness to your experience for a few moments.
- Bring to mind the situation that is making you feel stuck. Rather than getting pulled into the storyline, take a moment to notice and acknowledge the emotions, thoughts, and sensations that are arising. Gently take note, knowing there is nothing you need to do about it.
- See whether you can detect what striving feels like in the body. Notice any holding, tension, or tightness. Focus your attention on the sensations, aware of their size and quality and of any movement. As you focus, practice breathing directly into and out from the sensations. Imagine your breath making space for whatever is here.

(CONTINUED)

- As you breathe, try offering yourself these phrases:

  It is okay to feel this

  It is already here

  I can make space for this, and there is no need to fix it

  Let me welcome this with compassion

- Continue to offer yourself these phrases as you attend to where this resistance shows up in the body.
- As this practice comes to an end, take a moment to feel the whole body, letting it be just as it is.

82. LETTING GO, HOLDING TIGHT

🕐 20 minutes 🖊 pen and paper

When stuck in depression, we often feel unmotivated. Things that used to interest us or bring us pleasure start to seem like chores. As we withdraw, our mood worsens. One of the things that makes it hardest to re-engage is our prediction that we won't enjoy that walk or that the coffee date will only make us feel worse. With non-striving, we can let go of the outcome and bring a sense of interest to the process. Rather than getting dragged down into the spiral of depression, we can hold tight to ourselves while depression passes.

- For this practice, you will need a paper and pen. Find a quiet place where you can complete this practice.
- First, take a few minutes to reflect, and then write down five activities that give you a sense of mastery. These are activities or tasks that give you a sense of accomplishment or pride. See whether you can pick something small or one step of a larger project, like opening a few pieces of mail, clearing off a section of your desk, folding some laundry, or going for a short walk.

- Next, take a few minutes to reflect, and then write down five activities that give you a sense of pleasure. These are activities that you find soothing or enjoyable. See whether you can pick something easily accessible, like cuddling with a pet, taking a shower, or having a cup of tea.
- Take a moment to notice your experience. What are you noticing in body and in mind? Choose one of these ten activities, and see whether you can complete it with a sense of beginner's mind. Bring your full attention to it, and focus on the process without any expectations about whether you will enjoy it or feel better afterward.
- If unhelpful thoughts arise that this activity should be easy or isn't worth your efforts, gently note the thoughts and bring your attention back to the activity.
- When you are finished, take a moment to notice again what you are experiencing in body or mind. Regardless of whether this "helped" you, congratulate yourself for working wisely with your mood.
- When you feel stuck or stagnant, see whether you can choose another activity from your list to complete in this way.

83. CONNECT WITH PURPOSE

🕐 10 minutes

When we are overly attached to an outcome or goal, we end up with our emotions tethered to forces that may be out of our control. Despite our best efforts, sometimes things don't turn out our way. Yet when we focus on the why, or the value behind the goal, we can see how our behavior is important regardless of the outcome. This way we connect with a purpose deeper than success or failure.

(CONTINUED)

- Adopt a comfortable and dignified posture. You can gently close your eyes or cast your gaze downward.
- Now take a minute to feel the sensations of sitting here. Connect with any points of touch or contact in the body as you arrive in this moment.
- Take a few minutes to settle your attention on the breath. Closely and carefully attend to the sensations of the breath coming in and out, wherever you feel it most clearly.
- Bring to mind an area of your life where you find striving, clinging, or attachment. Maybe this is achievement at work, goals around your physical body, or ambitions in your home life. Allow this area to enter your mind, and acknowledge the goals or outcomes that you are clinging to.
- Let go of thinking and notice where this affects you in the body. Gently scan the body and see whether you can detect any areas of tightness, pressure, or discomfort. For a few moments, see whether you can breathe with any discomfort that arises, really feeling it and making space for it to be here. Gently acknowledge that *this is striving*.
- Take a moment to reflect on what's behind this goal. Why is it important? What in your life do you really care about that this goal would help with? Continue to focus on your breath as an anchor as you pose questions to yourself. Keep asking yourself *why?* Make note of the ways this goal reveals your values, regardless of whether you achieve it.
- As you complete this practice, take a moment to return to the breath. Whatever arose for you, take a moment to appreciate your efforts to see a bigger purpose.

84. FORGETTING FIXING

🕐 10 minutes

The desire for things to be a certain way can be a powerful force in our relationships with others. Our efforts to fix or change the people in our lives can be one of the greatest sources of suffering for both us and them. If you imagine the adversarial relationship that striving creates in ourselves, think about how this behavior affects how we treat others. Noticing how we strive to control others can help us unhook from these destructive efforts and become more present in our relationships.

- Start this practice by finding a comfortable and quiet place to sit. Adopt a posture that feels awake and open. You can perform this practice with your eyes open or closed.
- Take a few minutes to simply follow the sensation of breathing. Know that all you have to do for this moment is feel the breath. When you notice your mind has wandered, simply guide it back to the breath.
- When you are ready, bring to mind a relationship that you wish to preserve, protect, or nourish, but in which there is some struggle. Take a moment to reflect on the ways you may be trying to control or change this person. Notice any ways you want them to be different than they are. Simply breathe with awareness as you acknowledge it.
- Take a few deeper breaths to center yourself, and see whether you can gently invite acceptance of this person exactly as they are. With each round of breath, allow any effort to recede, and simply be with things as they are. See whether you can hold any sensations that arise in an open and allowing awareness. Continue to breathe in this way for a few minutes, cultivating an attitude of non-striving about this relationship.

(CONTINUED)

- Finally, ask yourself the following questions: *How can I approach this relationship with an attitude of non-striving? What would it be like to let go of needing this person to be different?* Rather than getting caught up in thinking, see whether you can allow these inquiries to simply settle into the mind and listen for whatever arises.
- As this practice comes to an end, take a moment to appreciate your efforts to forget fixing.

85. SLEEP TIGHT
(Mini-Meditation)

When you get into bed at night, take a moment to settle in and just notice what it feels like to lie here. Feel where your body meets the bed. Tune in to the sensations of the blankets and sheets as you let the body be supported by the bed. If you notice any sensations of gripping or holding, take a few deeper breaths, letting go to the degree you can on the exhale. Remind yourself there is nothing left to do now but sleep.

86. FINDING GRACE

🕐 10 minutes

Aspirations can motivate us to make difficult changes. The problem arises when our ideas about how things "should be" create suffering, including self-judgment. Danna Faulds puts it this way in her poem "Allow":

> *Resist, and the tide*
> *will sweep you off your feet.*
> *Allow, and grace will carry*
> *you to higher ground.*

Self-compassion is key to finding grace. In this practice, we move through the three components of self-compassion as described by Kristin Neff.

- Adopt a posture that feels comfortable and awake to the present moment. Allow any obvious areas of tightness or tension to gently relax. Maybe let your shoulders, jaw, and belly loosen. Either close your eyes or cast your gaze softly on the floor.
- Take a few deeper breaths to allow the body and mind to settle. Then allow the breath to resume its natural rhythm.
- When you are ready, bring to mind an area of striving or stress in your life that causes you to be hard on yourself.
- First, spend a moment being aware of what you notice. Gently acknowledge any thoughts, emotions, or bodily sensations that arise with this striving. Perhaps offer silently to yourself:

> *This is a moment of suffering*
>
> *Ouch*
>
> *This hurts*
>
> *This is hard*

(CONTINUED)

- Second, spend a moment acknowledging the common humanity in this experience. Perhaps offer silently to yourself:

  Suffering is part of life

  We all struggle in our lives

  There are others who feel this way, too

  I am not alone

- Third, spend a moment cultivating self-kindness. Perhaps place a hand on your heart or somewhere else that feels comforting and repeat silently to yourself:

  May I learn to accept myself as I am

  May I hold myself in compassion

  May I be kind to myself

  May I offer myself grace

- As this practice comes to an end, take the last few moments to reconnect with a sense of the body and the breath before returning your attention to the room.

Words of Encouragement

The patterns we are working to disentangle ourselves from are deeply ingrained. Attachment and aversion are part of being human. At the same time, these forces can easily sweep us into control mode. The more you can simply become aware of striving, the more you get out of autopilot and back into your life.

Reflection

What did you notice as you worked through these meditations? What aspects of your experience stood out? How can you apply the attitude of non-striving to your daily life?

Mindfulness Meditations for Depression

Letting go is the act of getting to know yourself

so deeply that all delusions fall away.

—*Yung Pueblo, writer and meditator*

CHAPTER EIGHT

Letting Go

In his lectures, the founder of mindfulness-based stress reduction, Jon Kabat-Zinn, tells the story of the clever way some farmers in India catch monkeys. According to Kabat-Zinn, the farmers cut a hole in a coconut, place a banana inside, and attach the contraption to a tree. Monkeys passing by reach inside the coconut to grab the banana—and soon realize they cannot remove their fist while holding the banana. In order to be free, all the monkeys have to do is let go of the banana. However, most monkeys will not release the banana. Thus they are stuck.

Like the monkeys, we often find ourselves clinging to something that is not serving us. In depression, this clinging shows up in how we respond to painful feelings. In other words, it is not the unpleasant feelings or sensations themselves but our relationship to them that keeps us stuck.

Letting go is a path to freedom. Rather than allowing sadness, tension, or anger at ourselves to pull us down, we can stop feeding the self-perpetuating pattern by allowing things to be as they already are. Like the monkeys, in order to survive, we have to loosen our grip. When we do this and remove our hand from the coconut, we make room to find something new that might nourish us even more than the banana. This way of moving through life's challenges is something we practice over and over, starting anew each time we are caught.

Common Unhelpful Thoughts

> *Something has to change.*
> *I can't handle this.*
> *This is impossible.*

---

87. RECEIVE AND RELEASE

🕐 5 minutes

Letting go often runs counter to our typical way of dealing with emotional pain. We become so consumed with fighting or fixing that we actually forget we can let go. One way to remember that letting go is always there for us is to practice it. Luckily, we are practicing it all the time without even knowing it. Every time the body receives a breath, it has to let it go.

- Begin this practice by finding a comfortable seat with your body upright and balanced. You can gently close your eyes or cast your gaze downward.
- As you settle in, take a moment to attend to your posture. Feel your chest open, and invite the body to relax to the degree that it will.
- Shift your focus to the sensations of the breath. Allow your attention to rest wherever the breath feels clearest or most pleasant to you.
- See whether you can allow the breath to be natural. There is no need to control or change it at all.

- As you breathe, see whether you can notice how the body receives the breath and softly releases it. The body knows how to let go.
- Whenever you become aware that your attention is no longer on the breath, gently take note of where the mind has gone, and then deliberately guide your attention back to the breath. Each time you do this, you are practicing letting go.
- Continue to follow the sensations of the breath as it is received and released by the body.
- As this practice comes to an end, gently open your eyes or expand your gaze as you take in your physical space.

---

88. OPEN TO THE SOUNDSCAPE

🕐 5 minutes

It is usually when we begin to acknowledge the unworkability of trying to control everything—encountering the suffering that resistance creates—that we realize we must let go. Letting go doesn't mean we don't want to change certain things. Instead, it focuses on our ability to recognize a situation clearly (including our desire for it to be different) without getting so stuck. Paying attention to sound can give us practice in opening up to things as they are and letting go of controlling.

- Find a comfortable seat and adopt a posture that allows your body to be upright and also relaxed. You can allow your eyes to gently close or cast your gaze downward.
- As you settle in, take a few moments to feel the sensations of sitting here. Notice the weight of the body and any points of touch or contact.
- Begin to attend to the breath wherever it feels clearest and most pleasant to you. Allow any thoughts to fade into the background as you carefully follow the sensations as the body breathes in and out.

(CONTINUED)

- Now, shift your attention from your breath to noticing the sounds happening around you. You don't need to do anything. For a few minutes, simply let go and allow sounds to arrive at the ears.
- Notice sounds arising in the field of your awareness and passing away. Relax into the soundscape, not opposing anything.
- If you become aware of judgments about these sounds, gently let go and open back up to receive the sounds around you.
- As this practice comes to an end, take a moment to return your attention to the sensations of the breath before slowly re-entering your day.

89. SEEING THE TRAP

🕐 15 minutes

When we are hyperfocused on physical or emotional discomfort, the rest of the world seems to fade from our awareness. We continue to dig ourselves deeper with the only tool we feel we have: thinking. When we let go, we can drop thinking and pick up a new tool that might actually get us out of the hole. As we maneuver out, we can see the bigger picture, the difficulty we are encountering, and how we relate to it. We see the trap. Try this meditation to help you open up to the bigger picture.

- Begin this practice by adopting an alert and relaxed posture. Gently close your eyes, or cast your gaze softly downward.
- Start to feel the body breathing. For a few minutes, carefully allow your attention to settle on the sensations of the breath.
- If you become aware that your attention has wandered back into thinking, see whether you can simply guide it back to feeling on the next inhale and the next exhale.
- Expand your attention to feel the body sitting here. Allow thinking to gently fade into the background, and if possible, gently allow your attention to move down from your head into the body. For a few minutes, just hold the whole body in a kind and spacious awareness.

- When you are ready, begin to explore the possibility of letting go of your focus on the breath and body, and open the awareness up to whatever arises in your experience.
- As you open up to the bigger picture, gently observe whatever arises in the body, heart, and mind and in the space around you. Allow it all to come and go in the space of awareness.
- Any time you find the mind has gotten pulled into thinking, storytelling, or remembering, gently let go. Notice any reactivity that arises, and see whether you can let go and open back up to an expansive awareness of the whole landscape of your experience.
- Rest in awareness, allowing it to unfold moment to moment.
- For the last few moments of this practice, allow your attention to narrow once again to the breath. Tune in to the sensations on the inhale and the exhale. Slowly open your eyes or widen your gaze to take in the space you're in.

90. GATHER AND LET GO
(Mini-Meditation)

Whenever you become aware of feeling unfocused or scattered, stop what you are doing and focus your attention on taking three deep breaths. Breathe in fully though your nose. Gather your attention as you feel the breath fill your body. Breathe out slowly through your mouth. As you exhale, see whether you can let go of thoughts or emotions that are no longer needed. Bring your full awareness to the length of three conscious and deep breaths before returning to your day. Remember that you can always return to your breathing to gather your attention and let go.

91. DISSOLVING

🕐 10 minutes

Letting go is a process. Rather than getting rid of negative thoughts or feelings, letting go is the practice of releasing our reactivity to them so we regain some perspective. When we can see our experience with a bit more distance, we leave room to see that, as author and meditation teacher Ruth King says, "Nothing in life is personal, permanent, or perfect." In this meditation, when we allow parts of our body to dissolve from awareness, we practice releasing the past and inviting a fresh perspective on the present.

* Begin this practice by finding a comfortable posture, either lying on your back on a mat or seated in a chair. If you are lying down, let your legs and arms be long, with your palms facing up and your feet falling away from each other. You can perform this practice with your eyes open or closed.
* To start, take a few moments to connect with the sensations of the body just as it is. Notice any points of contact or pressure where the body is held and supported by the surface you are on.
* When you are ready, start to attend to the sensations of the breath at the belly. As you feel your breath coming in and out, take a moment to reflect on your intention to be with the sensations in each region of your body. See whether you can investigate and let go of whatever arises as you move through this practice. Know that at any time, you can always return to the breath to steady yourself.
* Shift your attention down to the feet. Begin to observe any sensations in the feet. Notice any temperature, movement, or lack of sensation.
* On an exhale, allow the feet to dissolve from awareness. As you inhale, shift your attention to the legs. Feel into any sensations in the legs. Notice any pressure, fatigue, or ease.
* If you become aware that the mind has wandered, gently guide it back to the body and the sensations present in this moment.
* On an exhale, allow the legs to dissolve from awareness. As you inhale, shift your attention up to the pelvis, abdomen, and chest.

Feel into sensations arising from deep inside the body and from the surface of the skin.

- On an exhale, allow the pelvis, abdomen, and chest to dissolve from awareness. As you inhale, shift your attention to the arms and hands. Observe any moisture, heat, or coolness.
- On an exhale, allow the arms and hands to dissolve from your awareness. As you inhale, shift your attention to the face, neck, and shoulders. Feel into sensations of tension, holding, or softness.
- On an exhale, allow the face, neck, and shoulders to dissolve from your awareness. As you inhale, see whether you can expand your attention to include your whole body lying here.
- Allow a few minutes to breathe with the whole play of sensations in the body before slowly bringing some movement to your body and returning your awareness to the space you are in.

92. LET GO OF THE STORYLINE

🕐 10 minutes

One of the hardest habits to let go of is rumination. We encounter something unpleasant—a pain, an ache, a disappointment—and we are driven to start thinking about it. It can be compulsive. We create a whole storyline that takes us further and further from the truth of the difficulty. The momentum is so strong that we forget we don't have to believe our thoughts. In this meditation, we practice exiting this cycle.

- Start off this practice by finding a comfortable and alert seated posture. Allow your eyes to gently close, or cast your gaze softly in front of you.
- As you sit, begin to get in touch with the sensations where the body meets the surface you are sitting on and where the hands rest in your lap. Take a moment to sit and know that you are sitting.
- When you are ready, begin to attend to the breath. Allow your attention to simply rest wherever you feel the breath most clearly.

(CONTINUED)

- Carefully follow the full length of the inhale and the full length of the exhale.
- Now, for a few minutes, see whether you can bring a sense of curiosity to thinking as it happens. If thoughts that are highly charged arise or you find yourself pulled into thinking, you might use a more specific label like "self-critical thoughts" or "anxious thoughts." Kindly take note of the storyline and let it go.
- Know that as you practice breathing, noticing thoughts, and coming back to the breath, you are cultivating the ability to let go.

93. RECOGNIZE RESISTANCE

🕐 3 minutes

The opposite of letting go is resisting, grasping, and holding on. This impulse is a habit that often arises out of self-protection. We avoid the tenderness of sadness as we blame ourselves, or we forgo the intensity of our own anxiety as we find fault in others. Yet with practice, we can acknowledge these habits and caringly remind ourselves we no longer need them. When we shine light on our habitual patterns, they lose their grip on us. Meditation teacher Shaila Catherine says, "By understanding that the problem lies in the clinging, we learn to let go." Try this exercise when you become aware of difficulty or tension in your body or mind.

- Signify stepping into awareness by adopting a posture that is upright, alert, and relaxed. You can gently close your eyes or leave your eyes open.
- Take a minute to **turn your attention inward**. With an attitude of curiosity, take note of your experience in this moment. What sensations are present? Without needing to change anything, just notice how the body feels. What emotions are present? What thoughts are here? See whether you can observe without getting caught up.
- Once you have a sense of your experience, perhaps gently say to yourself, *This is what resistance feels like.*

- Allow a minute to let the mind settle, and **focus on your breath**. Bring your full attention to breathing, and if the mind wanders, gently guide it back.
- When you are ready, **expand your attention** to your body. Spend a minute holding the whole body in a kind awareness, allowing it to be just as it is.
- If you become aware of any remaining tension in the body, try sending the breath into and out from the sensations, investigating them and making space for them to be here. Perhaps remind yourself, *It's okay. Thank you for trying to protect me. I can feel this.*
- As this practice ends, see whether you can bring this tender, allowing awareness to the next moments of your day.

---

94. BREATHING OUT, LETTING GO

🕐 10 minutes

We are sent so many messages that we should always be happy that we come to think something is wrong if we feel sad, frustrated, or anxious. Sadness may bring up fears of impending depression, and anxiety may cause us to spiral into panic. But our unwillingness to experience these natural difficulties of being human doesn't stop the difficulty; it creates more distress and depletes our energy. When we can accept and allow discomfort, even for a moment, we step into the freedom of letting go.

- For this practice, adopt a posture that feels dignified and awake to the present moment. Let your hands rest easily on your lap, and allow your eyes to gently close.
- See whether you can gather your attention and arrive in this moment. Feel the points of contact where the body meets the surface you are sitting on.

(CONTINUED)

- When you are ready, shift your attention to feel the body breathing. For a few minutes, carefully feel the full length of the inhale and the full length of the exhale. Rest your attention on the sensations of the breath.
- Now take a moment to notice how the mind is in the moment. Is it busy or quiet? Open or contracted? Whatever you notice, see whether you can simply accept it and allow it to be however it is. Then, gently let it go.
- As you breathe in, invite acceptance and allowance, and as you breathe out, let go. Perhaps repeat *accepting, allowing* as you breathe in, and *letting go* as you breathe out.
- Now take a moment to notice how the body is in this moment. Take note of any sensations of tightness, heaviness, or holding. Whatever you notice, see whether you can kindly accept it and allow it to be that way. Then gently let it go.
- As you breathe in, invite acceptance and allowance, and as you breathe out, let go. Continue breathing in this way, repeating these phrases silently as you breathe in and out. Deepen your awareness and your attitude of letting go.
- Finally, spend a minute sitting in stillness, aware of the body and your breath.

95. DROPPING THE ROPE

🕐 10 minutes

When we feel stuck resisting the present moment, it's like we are playing tug of war with a monster at the bottom of a deep crater. As we grip the rope more tightly, the monster pulls us closer and closer to the edge. The more we attempt to resist, the more ground we lose. It's time to drop the rope. Trust that the pain won't last forever, and the energy spent fighting the monster is taking away from your ability to experience your life. Try this exercise as a regular practice, and integrate it when you notice this internal tug-of-war.

- Find a seated posture that feels relaxed and also open and alert. You can let your eyes gently close or cast your gaze softly downward.
- Take a minute to feel the weight of the body grounded on your seat or cushion. Also feel the body rising up and your chest open.
- Take a few fuller breaths. Breathe in deeply and let the breath go, sighing out audibly.
- After a few breaths, let the breath resume its natural rhythm, and feel the breath coming in and out.
- As you breathe in, bring your hands into a fist, squeezing them in. As you breathe out, release your hands, allowing them to softly open. Continue to breathe as you squeeze and release your hands.
- Attend to the sensations of holding on and letting go in the hands as you breathe.
- If your attention wanders or you find yourself pulled into thinking, guide your attention back to the sensations of holding on and letting go. Perhaps imagine that on the exhale, you are dropping the rope.
- For the last few moments of this practice, release any movement or effort and anchor the attention on your breath.
- If you find this exercise helpful, you can use it throughout the day to help you feel into letting go.

96. LOOSENING YOUR GRIP

© 10 minutes

Letting go can be hard because we think it means we are giving up, giving in, or saying the situation is okay. The truth is that letting go has nothing to do with our judgments about whether something is right or wrong. It also doesn't mean the difficulty is gone completely. Rather, it means we loosen our grip and release our efforts to fight reality. Christina Feldman and Jack Kornfield describe the damage we do to ourselves when we don't let go: "Anything that can be lost was never truly ours, anything that we deeply cling to only imprisons us."

(CONTINUED)

- Begin this practice by finding a posture that is alert, dignified, and relaxed. You can gently close your eyes or cast your gaze softly downward.
- Start by feeling a sense of being grounded here in this moment by feeling the body. Notice any points where the body meets the surface you are sitting on. Allow the body to settle.
- Let your attention shift from the body to the breath. Take a few minutes to simply feel the body breathing. See whether you can allow your attention to rest on your breath as it comes in and out of the body.
- When you feel ready, bring to mind a situation you have been resisting or fighting against. Take a moment to simply acknowledge the facts of the situation.
- See whether you can gently note any thoughts or judgments that arise without getting caught up in the story. Acknowledge any emotions that this difficulty brings with it. Remind yourself that all of you is welcome and it is okay to feel this way.
- Turn your attention to the body to see where this difficulty is felt. Gently scan the body for any holding, tightness, or pressure. If you detect any difficult sensations, spend some time breathing into and out from them. Allow this to be a gesture of acknowledging and making space.
- As you allow these sensations to be here, perhaps tell yourself, *It is okay, this is already here, let me be with it.*
- If you get caught up in thinking about the difficulty, return to noticing how it feels in the body. Rather than trying to change the sensations, see whether you can hold them with gentleness.
- For the last few minutes of this practice, take a few deeper breaths in, and allow the body to sigh aloud on the way out. Let this signify your efforts to loosen your grip.

97. RECOGNIZING IMPERMANENCE

⊕ 10 minutes

We delay finding contentment in life. *I will worry about finding a partner when I get a real job. I will focus on my hobbies when I have more money.* We can spend our whole lives striving as we prepare for some better and brighter future when we'll be happy. For me, my mom's cancer diagnosis woke me up to the madness of this approach. The truth is that we are only guaranteed this moment. If we allow it, the recognition of life's fragility and impermanence can help us let go and participate in our lives now.

- Find a comfortable seated posture. Allow your spine to be erect and also relaxed. You can gently close your eyes or cast your gaze softly downward.
- Spend a few moments getting in touch with the sensations of sitting. Tune in to how it feels where the body meets the chair or cushion, and sense the weight of the body grounded here.
- Start to pay attention to the breath. See where you feel the breath most clearly, and allow the attention to rest there.
- When you are ready, take a few moments to consider what you find yourself putting off, putting on hold, or sacrificing in your life until some future goal is met.
- Take a few deeper breaths to allow the mind to settle. Begin to contemplate what you want your life to be about, rather than specific goals to accomplish. Imagine yourself old and looking back on your life. What would matter most?
- Finally, reflect on how you might approach today differently if you let go of striving and allowed your actions to be guided by your deepest intentions for life.
- As this practice comes to an end, consider this quote by Ram Dass: "Our journey is about being more deeply involved in life, and yet less attached to it."

98. WORKING WITH ANGER

🕐 10 minutes

Working with anger is fertile ground for letting go. With mindfulness, we can start to see the various layers of our experience, including how reactions to painful experiences often fuel anger. The Buddha described this as being hit with two arrows. The first arrow, the initial event itself, is the painful experience. The second arrow is the one we shoot at ourselves: It is our clinging, perhaps to the need to be right or feel powerful. By paying attention to smaller irritations, fears, or frustrations, we can start to see the first arrow more clearly before it becomes anger.

- Begin this practice by finding a posture that embodies a sense of dignity and being awake. Allow your body to relax to the degree it will, softening the brow, the shoulders, and the belly. You can gently close your eyes or cast your gaze softly downward.
- Start by feeling the body grounded here in this moment. Establish a solid base by feeling the sensations of sitting here for a few moments.
- Once you feel grounded, bring to mind a current irritation, frustration, or hurt. Allow it to be in your mind for a moment, and start to take note of what thoughts arise in the mind and what emotions are present when you consider this situation.
- Then take a moment to attend to any sensations of contraction, holding, or tightness in the body. Allow your attention to kindly rest with what you feel in the body. Sense whatever is present and allow it to be there.
- As you acknowledge this discomfort in your body, see whether you can acknowledge any hurt or unmet need in yourself. What might be the first arrow? What do you need most? Is it perhaps to feel understood, cared for, appreciated, or safe?
- Now see whether you can bring a sense of awareness and kindness to that need. Perhaps place a hand gently on the body and offer a wish of compassion for whatever is needed. Continue to breathe as you recognize and care for whatever vulnerability you feel.

- As this practice comes to an end, allow yourself a few moments to feel the body once again. Gently hold the whole body and breathe in your awareness before slowly opening your eyes or widening your gaze.

99. LOCATING THE FIRE

🕐 10 minutes

In our efforts to avoid painful emotions, we often develop unhelpful habits that keep us stuck. These habits become so automatic that we fail to recognize what prompted them, as if we are running around turning off fire alarms without even knowing where the fire is. With mindfulness, we can learn to respond instead of react: We can notice the alarm going off, acknowledge the urge to shut it off, and turn our attention to instead locating the fire and avoiding adding fuel to the fire. Rather than let these habits overpower us, we can turn them into opportunities to wake up.

- See whether you can notice when an unhelpful habit starts to kick into gear. Maybe you find yourself wanting to eat when you are not hungry, nap even when you got enough sleep, or fall into self-criticism.
- Start by adopting an alert posture with your body. Allow your spine to be straight, let your shoulders relax, and perhaps gently close your eyes.
- Try to take a moment to simply notice that the alarm is going off rather than rushing to turn it off. Notice the landscape of your experience in this moment. What is here? Notice and gently label any thoughts, emotions, or sensations.
- Once you have a sense of your experience in this moment, see whether you can take a few deeper breaths and kindly let it be. Nothing to fix or solve here.
- Gently investigate the situation. Where is the fire? What is here? What pain or discomfort is here that wants my attention? Rather than thinking about this, see whether you can bring your attention to the body and detect any holding, resistance, or heat.

(CONTINUED)

- Perhaps bring a comforting hand to the body and ask yourself, *What is needed in this moment to address my pain or discomfort? How can I best take care of myself while this fire burns out? What is a response I can choose that would be kind, helpful, and wise?*
- As this practice ends, see whether you can move forward with your full awareness.

100. INVITING THE WIND TO BLOW

🕐 10 minutes

Letting go is not something we can force. It is like waiting for the wind to blow. We can only work to create the conditions for the letting go to happen. First, we can shine the light of awareness on our clinging. Second, when aversion tells us an experience will last forever, we can remember that nothing is permanent. Finally, if these steps open the door, self-compassion can invite the wind of letting go to blow through.

- Find a comfortable, awake, and dignified posture. You can either close your eyes or cast your gaze softly downward.
- Take a few minutes to settle into the present moment, attending to the body sitting here and the breath coming in and out. Allow your attention to ride on the waves of the breath.
- When you feel relatively settled, bring to mind a person or a pet in your life who loved or loves you unconditionally. Picture this person in your mind's eye, and allow yourself to rest in the warmth and care of this person's love for you. Even if you are not feeling deserving or worthy, recognize that their love for you is there. Feel their love for you just as you are.
- Now allow yourself to become the source as well as the object of these feelings. Perhaps feel your breath and the region of your heart as you say to yourself inwardly:

May I be safe from inner and outer harm

May I live with ease and happiness

May I be healthy and whole to whatever degree possible

May I be awake to my life just as it is

- Continue to repeat these phrases to yourself, allowing them to be felt fully. If your mind wanders off, gently guide it back to your breath and these phrases.
- When you are ready, imagine someone who is easy for you to love. This can be a person or a pet. For a few minutes, hold them in your mind's eye as you send these messages of love and warm wishes to this person:

  May you be safe from inner and outer harm

  May you live with ease and happiness

  May you be healthy and whole to whatever degree possible

  May you be awake to life just as it is

- Now let go of any particular phrases or focus of attention, and allow your attention to rest on the sensations of the body sitting here. Take a few moments to rest with the compassion you have cultivated. Even if this practice felt stiff or awkward at times, congratulate yourself for inviting the wind to blow.

Words of Encouragement

Letting go is a far cry from giving up or condoning behavior of which you disapprove. Rather, it is bearing the truth of the moment with courage and grace. With time, mindfulness allows us to skillfully meet what life offers us. It allows us to release expectations that ultimately cause us pain. Mindfulness is a process, not a destination. In each moment we calibrate (and re-calibrate) our compass in the direction of letting go.

Reflection

What did you notice as you worked through these meditations? What aspects of your experience stood out? How can you apply the attitude of letting go to your daily life?

Meditation practice isn't about trying to throw ourselves away and become something better. It's about befriending who we are already.

—Pema Chödrön, Buddhist teacher and author

CHAPTER NINE

Ongoing Self-Compassion

Mindfulness allows us to pay attention to the habitual patterns that leave us vulnerable to depression. By bringing compassionate awareness to the present moment, we can become alert to our unique early warning signs—the thoughts, emotions, sensations, and behaviors that indicate depression is arising.

Although we cannot wish away our thoughts and emotions, we can change the way we meet them. When we approach these thoughts and emotions with care and steadiness, we create room for wisdom. Choosing actions that are genuinely kind is not always easy, but it forms the basis for the truest form of self-care. Remember, mindfulness is meant to help us step out of self-critical spirals; it is not another reason to beat ourselves up. To avoid this trap, we must continually integrate compassion into our practice.

Our lives are busy and often tumultuous in ways that exert a strong pull toward autopilot and divided attention. It is easy to get swept away into our "to-dos" and "shoulds." Maintaining awareness takes a deliberate and steadfast commitment. To me, this means a regular mindfulness practice, however short. It is a critical base upon which to build other practices to address difficult emotions or behavioral patterns and to cultivate loving-kindness.

In order for our actions to be driven by our intentions for how we want to live our lives rather than the momentum of old patterns, we have to find a way to *practice* mindfulness.

Luckily, we can apply the same attitudes we have been cultivating throughout this book to create a pattern of practice that will support awareness. This means looking inward to determine what is truly manageable and starting there. Notably, mindfulness is not a quick fix. Much like you can't turn a huge ship in one fell swoop, you won't change your perspective overnight. Sustained small movements in a (mostly) consistent direction, while allowing yourself grace, will be the way toward a new shore.

Among the practices you have done so far, consider which will be most helpful for you going forward. This doesn't always mean picking what is easiest or your "favorite," but instead choosing practices that will provide the most clarity, well-being, and wisdom given your present needs. If we think of mindfulness as a muscle, we need to have regular conditioning so we can lift the heavy weights of life when we need to.

DAILY AWARENESS

This book was designed to give you the skills to approach your experience with attitudes that will support your mood and well-being. Pick an amount of time that is realistic for you to practice on a daily basis. The "everyday-ness" is going to help you establish a practice and awareness that promote an ability to shift into the "being mind" when needed.

Treat mindfulness the way you would other important health habits. We don't brush our teeth once in a day, say we are done for the week, and expect to have good oral hygiene. Linking a mindfulness practice with a place and time can help clear the path for a new habit to form. It is often useful to set a tiny, almost absurdly small goal when we are trying to form a new habit. For mindfulness, this may look like setting a goal of meditating for only one minute every day when you wake up, or purposefully bringing your full awareness to your morning when you drink a cup of coffee. You may want to set a goal of doing just one of the mini-meditations in this book each day. If you exceed your goal, that's wonderful, but just a minute is the tiny goal. As meditating becomes part of your routine, you'll tend to do longer practices.

We need to be flexible with ourselves and know that mindfulness is not just about sitting in meditation. It is about the awareness we bring to our daily lives. During the day, can you come back to feel your body and your feet on the ground? Can you notice when you are clenching your jaw and gently feel your breath and let go? As you establish the nuts and bolts of your ongoing practice, it's important to always apply an attitude of gentleness to yourself. As Tara Brach puts it, "This revolutionary act of treating ourselves tenderly can begin to undo the aversive messages of a lifetime."

Finally, knowing our "why" for practicing can bolster our ability to practice consistently. Perhaps we practice for greater ease, connection, clarity, or understanding. Rather than goals to be achieved, these values and aspirations can be a source of steady motivation that remain on the horizon as we look out and see the many obstacles to taking the time to practice. Even if we veer off course, we can still look out in front of us to remember our values and recalibrate our path.

THE MINDFUL WAY

The tools introduced here are the building blocks for us to mindfully respond to difficulty rather than to automatically react in ways that add to our suffering. These attitudes support a new approach to meeting our experience. We allow ourselves to know the nature of the difficulty so we can address it most skillfully.

Sometimes, a clear path of wise action may emerge from paying attention. Other times, we are faced with inner or outer circumstances that we cannot change. In these situations, the various ways that we try to control reality only add to a sense of depletion, hopelessness, and depression. Each of the mindful attitudes we have discussed here creates room for us to hold fast to ourselves and regain the power of choice. Rather than fighting, we can choose to accept the situation as it is, including our reactions to it. In making this choice, we decrease the odds that depression will take hold and nourish our relationship to ourselves.

By taking the mindful way, we learn that even in the face of difficulty, we can tap into the wisdom, courage, and goodness that is already within us. It is possible to achieve solace, time and again.

RESOURCES

BOOKS

Brach, Tara. *Radical Acceptance: Embracing Your Life with the Heart of a Buddha*. With a foreword by Jack Kornfield. New York: Bantam Books, 2003.

Chödrön, Pema. *When Things Fall Apart: Heart Advice for Difficult Times*. Shambhala Classics. Boston: Shambhala Publications, 1997.

Germer, Christopher K. *The Mindful Path to Self-Compassion: Freeing Yourself from Destructive Thoughts and Emotions*. With a foreword by Sharon Salzberg. New York: Guilford Press, 2009.

Gunaratana, Henepola. *Mindfulness in Plain English*. Boston: Wisdom Publications, 1991.

Hanh, Thich Nhat. *The Miracle of Mindfulness: An Introduction to the Practice of Meditation*. Translated by Mobi Ho. Boston: Beacon Press, 1976.

Kabat-Zinn, Jon. *Wherever You Go, There You Are: Mindfulness Meditation in Everyday Life*. New York: Hyperion, 1994.

Kornfield, Jack. *The Wise Heart: A Guide to the Universal Teachings of Buddhist Psychology*. New York: Bantam Books, 2008.

Neff, Kristin. *Self-Compassion: The Proven Power of Being Kind to Yourself*. New York: Harper Collins, 2011.

Orsillo, Susan M., and Lizabeth Roemer. *The Mindful Way through Anxiety: Break Free from Chronic Worry and Reclaim Your Life*. With a foreword by Zindel V. Segal. New York: Guilford Press, 2011.

Salzberg, Sharon. *Lovingkindness: The Revolutionary Art of Happiness*. With a foreword by Jon Kabat-Zinn. Boston: Shambhala Publications, 1995.

Williams, Mark, John Teasdale, Zindel Segal, and Jon Kabat-Zinn. *The Mindful Way through Depression: Freeing Yourself from Chronic Unhappiness*. New York: Guilford Press, 2007.

GUIDED MEDITATIONS

Kristen Neff: Self-Compassion.org/category/exercises/#guided-meditations

Susan M. Orsillo and Lizabeth Roemer: MindfulWayThroughAnxiety.com/exercises

Tara Brach: TaraBrach.com/guided-meditations

University of California, San Diego, Center for Mindfulness: MedSchool.UCSD.edu/som/fmph/research/mindfulness/programs/mindfulness-programs/MBSR-programs/Pages/audio.aspx

APPS

Calm: Calm.com
Headspace: Headspace.com
Insight Timer: InsightTimer.com

REFERENCES

Blake, William. *The Complete Poetry and Prose of William Blake*. Rev. ed. Edited by David V. Erdman. With commentary by Harold Bloom. New York: Anchor Books, 1988.

Brach, Tara. *Radical Acceptance: Embracing Your Life with the Heart of a Buddha*. With a foreword by Jack Kornfield. New York: Bantam Books, 2003.

Brody, Debra J., Laura A. Pratt, and Jeffery P. Hughes. *Prevalence of Depression among Adults Aged 20 and Over: United States, 2013–2016*. NCHS Data Brief, no. 303. Hyattsville, MD: Centers for Disease Control and Prevention, National Center for Health Statistics, 2018.

Catherine, Shaila. *Focused and Fearless: A Meditator's Guide to States of Deep Joy, Calm, and Clarity*. Boston: Wisdom Publications, 2008.

Chah, Ajahn. *Being Dharma: The Essence of the Buddha's Teachings*. Translated by Paul Breiter. With a foreword by Jack Kornfield. Boston: Shambhala Publications, 2001.

Chah, Ajahn. *A Still Forest Pool: The Insight Meditation of Achaan Chah*. Compiled by Jack Kornfield and Paul Breiter. Wheaton, IL: Quest Books, 1985.

Chödrön, Pema. "Meditating with Emotions: Drop the Story and Find the Feeling." *Tricycle* 22, no. 4 (Summer 2013). Tricycle.org/magazine /meditating-emotions.

Chödrön, Pema. *When Things Fall Apart: Heart Advice for Difficult Times*. Shambhala Classics. Boston: Shambhala Publications, 1997.

Chödrön, Pema. *The Wisdom of No Escape: And the Path of Loving-Kindness*. Shambhala Library. Boston: Shambhala Publications, 2010.

Dass, Ram. *One-Liners: A Mini-Manual for a Spiritual Life*. New York: Bell Tower, 2002.

The Enlightened Heart: An Anthology of Sacred Poetry. Edited by Stephen Mitchell. New York: Harper Perennial, 1993.

Faulds, Danna. *Go In and In: Poems from the Heart of Yoga*. Kearney, NE: Morris Publishing, 2002.

Frankl, Viktor E. *Man's Search for Meaning: An Introduction to Logotherapy*. 4th ed. Part One translated by Ilse Lasch. With a preface by Gordon W. Allport. Boston: Beacon Press, 1992.

Hanh, Thich Nhat. *Being Peace*. With an introduction by Jack Kornfield. Rev. ed. Edited by Rachel Neumann. Berkeley, CA: Parallax Press, 2005.

Hanh, Thich Nhat. *Happiness: Essential Mindfulness Practices*. Berkeley, CA: Parallax Press, 2009.

Hanh, Thich Nhat. *Living Buddha, Living Christ*. 20th anniversary ed. With an introduction by Elaine Pagels and a foreword by David Steindl-Rast. New York: Riverhead Books, 2007.

Hanh, Thich Nhat. *Love Letter to the Earth*. Berkeley, CA: Parallax Press, 2013.

Kabat-Zinn, Jon. *Full Catastrophe Living: Using the Wisdom of Your Body and Mind to Face Stress, Pain, and Illness*. 15th anniversary ed. New York: Delta, 2005.

Kabat-Zinn, Jon. *Wherever You Go, There You Are: Mindfulness Meditation in Everyday Life*. New York: Hyperion, 1994.

King, Ruth. *Mindful of Race: Transforming Racism from the Inside Out*. Boulder, CO: Sounds True, 2018.

Knaster, Mirka. *Discovering the Body's Wisdom: A Comprehensive Guide to More than Fifty Mind-Body Practices That Can Relieve Pain, Reduce Stress,* and Foster Health, Spiritual Growth, and Inner Peace. New York: Bantam Books, 1996.

Kornfield, Jack. The Wise Heart: A Guide to the Universal Teachings of Buddhist Psychology. New York: Bantam Books, 2008.

Lampert, Noah. "Faith and Meditation." Real Happiness Meditation Challenge (blog). February 3, 2015. SharonSalzberg.com/faith-meditation.

Lao Tzu. Tao Te Ching: The Book of the Way. Translated by Dwight Goddard. Revised by Sam Torode. Ancient Renewal. Nashville, TN: Sam Torode Book Arts, 2009.

Lao Tzu. Tao Te Ching: A New English Version. Translated by Stephen Mitchell. Modern Classics. New York: Harper Perennial, 1988.

Lao Tzu. The Way of Life According to Lao Tzu: An American Version. Translated by Witter Bynner. New York: Perigee Books, 1986.

Little, Tias. "Working with Difficult Emotions in Yoga." Yoga International. Accessed July 24, 2020. YogaInternational.com/article/view/working -with-emotions-in-yoga.

Neff, Kristin. Self-Compassion: The Proven Power of Being Kind to Yourself. New York: Harper Collins, 2011.

Ogden, Pat, Kekuni Minton, and Clare Pain. Trauma and the Body: A Sensorimotor Approach to Psychotherapy. With forewords by Daniel J. Siegel and Bessel A. van der Kolk. New York: W.W. Norton, 2006.

Oliver, Mary. Swan: Poems and Prose Poems. Boston: Beacon Press, 2010.

Orsillo, Susan M., and Lizabeth Roemer. The Mindful Way through Anxiety: Break Free from Chronic Worry and Reclaim Your Life. New York: Guilford Press, 2011.

Pueblo, Yung (yung_pueblo). "Old patterns do not give up easily." Instagram photo, June 18, 2020. Instagram.com/p/CBlG-dSjRPx.

Rogers, Carl. *On Becoming a Person: A Therapist's View of Psychotherapy*. With an introduction by Peter D. Kramer. New York: Mariner Books, 1995.

Rumi, Jalal al-Din. *The Essential Rumi: New Expanded Edition*. Translated by Coleman Barks, with John Moyne, A. A. Arberry, and Reynold Nicholson. San Francisco: Harper Collins, 2004.

Sahn, Seung. "Not Just a Human World." *Kwan Um School of Zen Teaching Library*. May 31, 1990. KwanUmZen.org/teaching-library/1990/06/01/not-just-a-human-world.

Salzberg, Sharon. *Lovingkindness: The Revolutionary Art of Happiness*. With a foreword by Jon Kabat-Zinn. Boston: Shambhala Publications, 1995.

Salzberg, Sharon. *Real Happiness: The Power of Meditation*. New York: Workman Publishing, 2011.

Segal, Zindel V., J. Mark G. Williams, and John D. Teasdale. *Mindfulness-Based Cognitive Therapy for Depression*. 2nd ed. With a foreword by Jon Kabat-Zinn. New York: Guilford Press, 2013.

Stories of the Spirit, Stories of the Heart: Parables of the Spiritual Path from Around the World. Edited by Christina Feldman and Jack Kornfield. San Francisco: Harper San Francisco, 1991.

Substance Abuse and Mental Health Services Administration. *Results from the 2011 National Survey on Drug Use and Health: Mental Health Findings*. NSDUH Series H-45, HHS Publication No. (SMA) 12-4725. Rockville, MD: Substance Abuse and Mental Health Services Administration, 2012.

Suzuki, Shunryu. *Zen Mind, Beginner's Mind: Informal Talks on Zen Meditation and Practice*. 50th anniversary ed. Edited by Trudy Dixon. With a preface by Huston Smith, an introduction by Richard Baker, and an afterword by David Chadwick. Boston: Shambhala Publications, 2020.

Teasdale, John, Mark Williams, and Zindel Segal. *The Mindful Way Workbook: An 8-Week Program to Free Yourself from Depression and Emotional Distress*. With a foreword by Jon Kabat-Zinn. New York: Guilford Press, 2014.

Tolle, Eckhart. *A New Earth: Awakening to Your Life's Purpose*. 10th anniversary ed. New York: Penguin Books, 2016.

Tolle, Eckhart. *The Power of Now: A Guide to Spiritual Enlightenment*. Paperback ed. Novato, CA: New World Library; Vancouver: Namaste, 2004.

Watts, Alan W. *The Essence of Alan Watts*. Millbrae, CA: Celestial Arts, 1977.

Watts, Alan W. *The Wisdom of Insecurity: A Message for an Age of Anxiety*. With an introduction by Deepak Chopra. New York: Vintage Books, 2011.

INDEX

ABOUT THE AUTHOR

 Sophie Lazarus, PhD, is a clinical psychologist and a certified teacher of mindfulness-based cognitive therapy through the University of California, San Diego, Mindfulness-Based Training Institute. She is an assistant professor in Psychiatry and Behavioral Health at the Ohio State University Wexner Medical Center, where she is involved in research, training, and delivery of mindfulness-based and cognitive-behavioral interventions for depression and anxiety. She has a long-standing practice of insight and loving-kindness meditation and has dedicated her career to helping those struggling with mental illness achieve greater well-being and self-compassion.